ACCLAIM

"If laughter truly is the best medicine, then Dr. Margie Peppercorn has written a fantastic prescription in *Mrs. M.D.* Having spent a career as a pediatrician - while simultaneously raising her children and running what at times sounded like something between her own petting zoo and a 3-ring circus – she shares from an endless trove of hilarious mishaps and adventures that seemed to have been her daily life. But *Mrs. M.D.* is far more than a compilation of "kids say the darnedest things" and wacky animal tales.

It is an important reminder that it was not long ago that there were very few women in medicine and even fewer who juggled the rigors of medical training and running a practice with a desire to be present for her family, all at a time when the field of medicine (as with most other professions) did not always support these pursuits. Many of the personal experiences she relays fall far out of the realm of what we are taught how to deal with in medical school and range from the shocking (how does one deal with a male physician who feels more than comfortable making inappropriate comments while you're performing CPR in the ER?), to the harrowing (what advice do you give to a teen who has just given birth to a baby at home, alone?), to the downright absurd (how do you convince a lab technician at a pediatric hospital to run a diagnostic test… on your son's pet turtle?). And while she manages to touch on both the highs and lows of medicine, Dr. Peppercorn addresses the issues with such compassion and humor that I found myself smiling or laughing on almost every page. Whether you are a physician, or a working parent, or an animal lover, if you are looking for a highly entertaining read that you can relate to, *Mrs. M.D.* is just what the doctor ordered."

Daniel Gruenstein, M.D.
Pediatric Cardiologist

"This book gives the reader a unique and fascinating opportunity to walk in the footsteps a woman doctor at a time when women doctors were rare and often not acknowledged. With humor, vulnerability, and honesty, this powerful, engaging book brings us into the colorful funny life of a woman doctor trying to do it all while juggling the challenges and transparency of motherhood and a pediatric practice in a small town. I highly recommend this engrossing, passionate, humorous, and profoundly readable book!"

Barbara Zucker, Psychotherapist

———

"Read this delightful memoir! Even the chapter titles (e.g., "To Pee or Not to Pee") will make you smile as they invite you in. Margie Peppercorn has a keen eye for the absurd wherever she finds it...the Emergency Room, the kitchen, the pediatricians' office, the supermarket, the home, or the horse barn. And she shares it all with humor and affection."

Mort Birnbaum PhD, Clinical Child Psychologist, Formerly Psychiatry faculty Harvard Medical School and U Mass Medical School and Psychology faculty University of Michigan

———

"As a teacher, I thoroughly appreciate how Dr. Margie Peppercorn takes us on a sentimental, humorous, and insightful journey into the world of being a parent, pediatrician, animal rights advocate, and more!! This book is a delightful read full of poignant and humorous anecdotal stories for those of us who want to enjoy the companionship of our best travel partners through life – our children, our spouses, our parents, our grand-parents, and our pets! The term I would use for the body of work is "triumphant". I went through a full range of emotions, we've all had ups and downs along with challenges in life, but it is the courage and ability or resilience in this book that most resonates with me. I recommend this book and believe so many would benefit from this special read. If you care deeply about your profession or seek long-term happiness through your work and in life, then put this book on your required reading list. I laughed and cried and you will also!"

Monica Steinberg, Elementary School Teacher

"As a former elementary school teacher and later clinical social worker, I was eager to read Margie Peppercorn's new book. I wanted to learn about the world of children from the perspective of a highly competent pediatrician. I thought Margie's book could fill the gaps in my own knowledge of how children behave and also what it's like to be a pediatrician. Little did I know this book would answer my questions but also that I would be doubled over in laughter as I read hilarious descriptions literally "out of the mouths of children." While some of the scenes and experiences may be unique, many are familiar and all provoke feelings anyone who has ever been near a child will understand. To cite an example, the chapter entitled To Pee or Not To Pee had me in stitches even before I read it. Can you imagine comparing Shakespeare's profound question on existence to the mundane act of urinating? Yet we all can identify with the difficulty of peeing on demand. Margie's writing is skilled and easily accessible. She delivers her own experiences with honesty, sharp insight and a delectable sense of humor. I cannot wait for the sequel!"

Donna Freeman M.Ed, ACSW.

Mrs. M.D.

Margie Peppercorn

Publisher's Information

EBookBakery Books

Author contact: margpep@aol.com

ISBN 978-1-953080-32-5

© 2022 by Margie Peppercorn

ACKNOWLEDGMENTS

Thanks are given to my husband, Mark, for his constant encouragement during my writing of this book and his thoughtful proofreading and editing. Thanks are also given to those others who took time to read and comment on my manuscript: Dan Peppercorn, Jeff and Amanda Peppercorn, Mort Birnbaum, Donna Freeman, Danny Gruenstein, Monica Steinberg, and Barbara Zucker. Thanks also to my incredibly helpful publisher I. Michael Grossman who helped make my dream of this book become a reality.

DEDICATION

This book is dedicated to my family and in particular to my dad, George Bessin, who taught me that a love of learning and a sense of humor were two of man's greatest companions, to my grandmother, Anna Schaffer, who's warmth, intelligence, energy, and love of life until her death at 95 were inspirational; to my mother, Bernice Bessin, who was a wonderful role model with her sensitivity, optimism, boundless love of people, and compassion for animals; to my sister and best friend, Barbara Zucker who, although a hardworking mother herself, always stood ready to listen and help; and to my husband Mark and my sons Jeff and Dan who gave my life meaning and endured the chaos described in this book sharing my laughter and tears.

It is also dedicated to my wonderful daughter-in-law Amanda and my fabulous grandchildren Lizzy, David, and Jack who weren't there during the events described when this book was originally written but have since then brought new adventures and boundless joy to my life.

CONTENTS

INTRODUCTION

Who am I to write a book and why did I do it? This thought kept haunting me as I found myself writing down story after story to my husband's constant refrain of, "How many pages do you have now? You need at least a hundred pages to call it a book. How can you ever think of twenty more pages?" And a friend's queries of, "Am I in the book? Don't you remember the times out west when we had so much fun? They were funny enough for you to mention me in the book, weren't they?"

My first thought of writing a book though actually came the time I was reading my children a humorous book about family life. As my younger son wiggled his own loose tooth and listened to the book's story of the child with the loose tooth, he looked amazed and asked me if I had written the book about him. The story's situations did in fact sound so familiar that I realized that I really could have written that book. The more we read and the more we laughed, my son became convinced that I had, in fact, written the book but wondered how I had possibly gotten it printed so quickly since some of the events had happened to us just that day.

I next thought about writing a book during an excursion with friends to view the fall foliage in Vermont. On arrival, after a tedious three hour drive, we discovered that as usual we had missed peak season and that the leaves had in fact been more colorful back home. We turned around and I spent the long three hour return trip trying to keep the driver awake by relating many of the stories on these pages.

Further thoughts of writing this book came at my office when the umpteenth mother asked me to tell her daughter briefly what it was like to be a doctor and the umpteenth patient asked to spend a sample day with me to see what medicine was all about. As you will soon discover there was no quick way to answer their questions or adequately describe my multiple lives as a woman and a doctor in any concise fashion since I realized that any description of my typical day could not simply start at the office but would have to start in the middle of the night or in our barn.

A tennis club near my house once advertised a special working woman's round robin for after work at 5:00pm. Every time I passed the sign I was struck by the fact that most men clearly had no idea what a working woman does. My friends and I agreed that to start after work, a tennis class for women would have to be held at midnight, after the office was closed, the dinner made and served, the children tucked in bed, the bills paid, and the wash done.

After spending a great deal of time contemplating maybe someday writing a book, what finally got me started and made it happen though were the close together deaths of my beloved grandmother and uncle. Those crushing sudden reminders of life's brevity made me decide that I had to stop ruminating about possibly writing a book some future day and needed to finally start putting these stories down on paper.

I'm hopeful that these pages will provide the reader with entertainment, some laughs, and a better understanding of the plight of working women since all of the events described are absolutely true with only minor changes in the characters' names to protect friends' and patients' privacy. As my son explained to his elementary school teacher at the time, "If you ever wanted to know what it is like to be a doctor, a mother, live in a zoo and lead a wild and woolly life, then this is the book for you."

WOMEN CAN BE DOCTORS

I WAS TOTALLY UNPREPARED FOR adulthood when I arrived. As a little girl I had played house occasionally but never with a real live husband who needed real live food and never with real live children who fought real live fights, fell out of trees and got real illnesses. I certainly had never played doctor with real middle-of-the-night calls from real patients with real worries and real illnesses. My parents, however, had brought me up to believe that I could do anything if I truly wanted to do it and tried hard enough.

Despite that philosophy I'm still unable to beat my husband in tennis but I did manage to graduate from a highly competitive medical school and become a pediatrician. There were certainly many difficulties along the way. My husband, a physician himself, thought the idea of women in medicine was terrific when he was merely my boyfriend. He wondered about whether or not women should be in medicine when he became my fiance, and then decided that women should definitely not be in medicine at all right after we were married. With both of us studying hard and working long hours I could readily agree with him that our household needed a "wife."

However, once my husband eventually realized that I couldn't be a fabulous cook no matter how many hours I was free to stand home at the stove and that, even if not at school or working, I could never keep a house as clean as his mother had, his convictions began to waver. When he later discovered that it was fun to be able to intelligently discuss our common medical careers he even became completely supportive.

That was not always true of the other male physicians I encountered. In the 60's when I went to medical school there were many fewer female physicians than there are now and we encountered many difficulties male physicians didn't. As a highly pregnant medical student, I not only had trouble fitting into the hospital elevator with my patients' stretchers but being pregnant also had trouble fitting into the expected role of standing attentively for long periods in the heavy scrub gowns and masks while watching or assisting surgeries. Several times after running up the stairs to reach the O.R. floor at the same time as my elevator-carried patient, I would arrive in surgery only to start feeling faint.

Male surgeons, ignoring my state of imminent birthing, would smugly tell me that they simply moved their legs during surgery to feel more alert and that since I was female, it was probably the sight of all that blood that was making me weak. On the two occasions that I did actually faint, surgical retractors in hand, they commented that I had at least had the medical sense to fall backwards and not in the way of the operative field so that the surgery could continue smoothly in my absence.

My being pregnant, however, did have its therapeutic advantages for some of my patients. I recall making rounds in a city hospital ward of sick elderly ladies who were all feeling ill, lonely, and sorry for themselves. They were each engrossed in their own suffering and none were paying any attention to the moans and groans of their neighbors. After I left the room though I could hear the atmosphere behind me brighten as the women temporarily forgot their current ailments and began talking to each other for the first time, commenting on the pregnant physician they had just seen and sharing stories of their own pregnancies and families.

At that time, being female and a physician also had other inherent difficulties unrelated to those of when I had been pregnant. Aside from having to learn to acquire a selective deafness to the suggestive remarks of some apparently all too healthy male patients or equally crude physicians, there was also the absence of female on-call rooms. The male physicians on duty had small bedrooms near the wards but during my nights on call I usually had to sleep on two chairs in the conference room or else in an empty bed on the women's ward. Several times when sleeping in the ward I would find myself wakened by the night nurse making rounds who assuming I was a patient had wanted to check my vital signs. Adjusting to these nights of minimal sleep proved to be excellent preparation, however, for future life both as a physician and as a mother.

Today most medical school classes are at least half women so people are used to dealing with female physicians but when I was in training most medical school classes were predominately male with less than 10 percent women. Since there were so few of us, many patients were unfamiliar with being examined by a woman and this sometimes posed a problem for some of the more shy male patients. I recall one bashful adolescent boy who came into the emergency room with what turned out to be a severely painful twisted testicle.

On arrival he took one look at the doctor on duty, who was me, and stated his ailment as headaches. As I carefully checked his eyes and ears he gradually relaxed enough to say his problem was actually chest pains. As I continued my examination by studying his heart and lungs he confided that his pains were really in his stomach. As I then intently examined his abdomen he finally felt brave enough to lower his stated area of complaint to the actual region of his illness.

Other patients had similar difficulties when arriving in the E.R. unfamiliar with the staff on duty. As their eyes glanced from my five foot three small frame and young face to the graying temples on the stout six foot two male orderly, they would sometimes ask me for a drink of water and the orderly for his medical advice.

One parent recognized that I was a physician but was still concerned because I was clearly fairly young and female. Just as I started to take the history of her child's illness she spotted the middle aged male orderly in the back of the examining room and very politely told me that she was sure I was a wonderful doctor but hoped I wouldn't mind if she asked the older gentleman in the room to examine her child instead of me. I told her that that would be fine with me if she wanted but that that gentleman was actually the orderly cleaning the room and not a doctor at all. She did then sheepishly agree to my treating her child and wound up pleased enough to return to see me for all of her child's follow up visits but in my early days of practice this sexism did remain an occasional problem and I even overheard a child once whisper quizzically to his mother that I hadn't been the doctor because I was just a "mommy."

Times change and experiences change however. It was therefore a thrill several years later to finally witness the long overdue recognition of women's place in medicine. A young girl who had been my patient since birth once had to see one of my male partners instead of me. It was the first time she had seen my partner and after he had finished examining her I happened to walk by his office just in time to overhear my patient's puzzled statement to her mother that they couldn't go home yet since she still hadn't seen the doctor because that person had been a man.

The difference of being a woman physician though did continue to often affect interactions with other physicians as well as patients. Male physicians often caught themselves as they started to ask me to pour the coffee for conferences or to be the recording secretary at meetings. Families select doctors for many different reasons but most often related to their expertise but teen age girls would occasionally come to me as patients solely because, "My mom just wanted me to see that women could be doctors."

Other parents chose me because they preferred a "mother" physician who they thought would be not only more understanding but also less threatening. This level of comfort and easy connection resulted in frequent calls to my house by parents who said they didn't think their question was important enough to disturb their own adult doctor on a Sunday but were sure I wouldn't mind. Other times parents would occasionally call me late at night saying they knew I wasn't on duty that night but they thought that I could advise them as to whether or not their child's symptoms were worrisome enough to bother my partner who they knew was the actual doctor on call.

Parents were right though that my being a mother myself did often make it easier to empathize with the anxieties of parents since I'd had to deal with my own children's illnesses. I also had had to deal with broken thermometers and refused, vomited or purposely spilled medication. I knew firsthand that the seemingly simple advice to sponge down a child's fever by putting him briefly into a tepid bath meant a frantic half hour of convincing or coercing a hysterically crying child into the cool water

4

resulting eventually in a dripping child, soaked mother, and drenched bathroom floor.

Being a mother in the town where I worked did result in increasingly frequent intrusions into my out of office life though. Trips to the grocery store were accompanied by whispered conversations of, "There's your doctor. See, she's buying broccoli too." Once parents realized that doctors might, in fact, need to sleep and eat like regular people, they often tried to see whether or not doctors really did sleep and eat like regular people as they peered into my shopping cart to see if it was crammed with health foods and fresh vegetables or whether it had candy, T.V. dinners and sugared cereals. Unrecognized ladies would approach me in the store with their toddlers in their grocery carts to ask me to listen to their child cough or suddenly stop me to ask me to tell their daughter to eat spinach.

Another problem with working in the town where I lived was that I was often under scrutiny even outside the grocery store. One of my sons once got a high powered rifle style water pistol as a gift from a friend. These were subsequently said to be unsafe for children so I put it on a shelf high out of reach meaning to later throw it away but promptly forgot about it.

Weeks later when in a rush to get to the store before my kids would be coming home from school I saw a raccoon staggering around our yard and then going under my car. I thought it might be sick and tried calling the town's animal control officer but couldn't reach anybody and really had to get to the store. Suddenly I remembered the water rifle, grabbed it and cautiously headed to the car with it. The raccoon was thankfully gone by the time I got there so I laid the water rifle on the seat and went to the store. Later in the grocery store parking lot I had the car door open to load my groceries into the car when a patient of mine and his mother happened to pull into the parking spot next to my car. The child had obviously just been arguing with his mother about getting one of those water guns because when he spotted the water rifle on the seat of my car he defiantly told his mother, "See, even Dr Peppercorn has one."

Having a large practice made it impossible for my office staff to instantly recall the names of the parents who infrequently needed to bring their children and only came for the yearly checkups. Nonetheless, on occasion our office secretary had intrusions into her own private life too. Sometimes a parent she couldn't recognize at all would see her in the grocery store and hand her a fistful of cash and say while rushing off that paying her child's bill there would save her from having to make a trip to the office.

In the past, doctors had always stood on pedestals, handing out dicta, right and wrong. I remember well the pediatrician I had used for my own children before I had completed my training. He was a wonderful, warm, caring man who nonetheless made motherhood a precise science. When my first baby was at the age to start solid food, my pediatrician made the pronouncement that I should give the baby one teaspoon of rice cereal on May 12 and add one teaspoon of applesauce on May 18.

Being a new mother I had no thoughts of questioning why the precise amounts or dates. I remember getting frantic on the evening of May 11 when I realized that the next day was time for cereal and that I had none in the house and the stores were all closed. My baby did well and grew into a healthy, intelligent child even though his cereal didn't start until May 13 and I eventually completed my motherhood and pediatric training but I never figured out the mystery of how or why my pediatrician had arrived at those precise dates for foods.

My patients faced a totally different medical experience. When they called me at night for advice on how to convince their two year old to stay in bed, they could hear mine laughing as he heard me on the phone and climbed out of his crib to play. When they called wanting advice on dealing with temper tantrums, they could hear my child screaming in the background because I was talking on the phone and not to him.

Even my friendly supermarket loomed as another arena to reveal my missing pedestal. One memorable day in the grocery store my youngest son decided to become a puppy. He followed my cart on all fours, barking and panting as I naturally met up with at least half a dozen patients. When I asked him to stop and sit up, he promptly sat on his hind legs in a begging posture and licked my leg. I recall that that night we had leftovers for supper as I decided my puppy needed a nap in his kennel more than I needed to complete my shopping.

The effects of having a mommy who was also a physician were also often heard in the play talk of my sons who had grown up immersed in hearing medical discussions. I'd hear one son play with all the abbreviations I used as he'd say he was "afebrile" and "asymptomatic" so he didn't need to go to the "ER" with his "URI" to get an "IV" or "LP" and see a "GI MD" about procedures in the "OR" or "ICU." My other son, an avid sports fan, developed his own unique athlete's understanding of medicine. One day as I began sneezing in his room while caring for him during one of his illnesses, I casually said that I thought I had caught his cold. At that point he looked at me quizzically and stated that I couldn't possibly have caught his cold because he still had it.

INTERNSHIP AND RESIDENCY

BEFORE BEING IN PRACTICE with the experiences as above however, I first had to complete my internship and residency. Internship and residency years have been depicted in many books and movies but few have accurately conveyed the panicky feeling of leaving behind the security of being a supervised student and crossing the threshold of a hospital emergency room as the new doctor on duty.

It is easy for many people though to appear calm and composed on the outside while actually being terrified on the inside. Some of us however have a subconscious quirk of appearance, movement, or speech that betrays our anxiety. In my case my anxiety used to manifest through my teeth. I had several fillings that would fall out of my mouth at times of stress. Dentists have been baffled and have tried replacing and recementing them but invariably at times of tension my fillings would fall out. I lost one at my first anatomy exam in medical school, one when starting my clinical clerkship, three before some surgery needed by my infant son, and two on my first day as an intern.

In any case, the big day finally arrived. I had my MD degree in hand and was on my own as a bonified doctor. The nurses at my internship hospital were very understanding and marvelously helpful. I recall one of my very first patients, a little girl with a bizarre body rash that had me totally mystified. As soon as she entered the examining room all knowledge of rashes flew right out of my head and I frantically stalled for time while trying to collect my wits by slowly examining her ears, throat, and belly. Eventually the nurse casually asked if I'd like her to get the Wood's lamp. I mumbled to her to of course please get it for me as I wracked my brain to remember what on earth a Wood's lamp was used for and what I should do with it when it arrived. Fortunately the appearance of the lamp landed me back on earth and brought back the recollection of the diagnostic fluorescence of ringworm rashes with such a lamp. The remainder of that first day in the E.R. thankfully went much more smoothly with the only notable event being the chaos created when a new teenage candy striper volunteer watching me suture a child's leg laceration took one look at the blood and fainted falling right through the treatment room curtain. The child's mother, who had previously been calmly waiting in the corridor outside saw the teenager faint through the curtain and began hysterically screaming that her poor child's wound was so dreadful that even the "nurse" had fainted.

The next few weeks held assorted problems dominated by the cataloging of all the intriguing items removed from children's ears and noses such as wads of paper, buttons, peas, small safety pins, beads, bugs, and erasers. Of course there were also the occasional true emergencies. I clearly recall the child who had had a cardiac arrest at home and had arrived by ambulance needing immediate attention and continued resuscitation. As the entire staff mobilized to treat this youngster, the tension was broken by the loud impatient complaints of the parent of another child waiting to be seen who demanded to know why her child still had to wait since she had been next in line ahead of the child who had just arrived. The tension of the scene was further punctuated by the lewd comments of one of the male physicians intent on discussing the rear view of a mini skirted female physician doing vigorous cardiac massage.

The E.R. was not the only stressful rotation at my hospital though. All interns had to rotate through nursery duty at an outlying hospital where at night we were the only pediatric physicians in the entire building and so had full responsibility for all newborns. Since the babies born were generally healthy, it eventually became easy to develop confidence. Disasters, however, occur without warning and it's hard to forget the feelings of the night when I suddenly heard the urgent page to report to the nursery STAT. In the nursery was a tiny blue 28-week premature infant who had been spontaneously born in bed and was now in an incubator with a very faint heartbeat and no independent respirations. Knowing that I was the only pediatrician within an hour of the nursery, I was extremely nervous but went to work with determination.

Suddenly the page sounded again with another STAT call for me to report to delivery. Assuming that the baby having difficulty in the delivery suite was probably more likely to survive than the one I was struggling with and knowing that I was the only pediatric doctor in the hospital, I left the head nurse in charge of bagging the first baby with oxygen and ran to the delivery room. There I received the shock that prompted another filling to fall from my mouth. The baby in delivery was the unexpected and critically ill identical twin of the premature infant already in the nursery. Somehow the nurses and I managed to revive and stabilize both babies and miracle of miracles saw them steadily grow over time and develop into normal healthy infants. The day that I received an invitation to their first birthday was one of the many rewarding joys that made me feel my career choice had been worthwhile.

Of course all experiences were not successes. I also recall having cared for a terminally ill little cancer patient and over the many months of his care having become very close with his mother. It was a dubious distinction and a surely humbling experience months later to be introduced to people at his funeral with "this was Davey's doctor."

Some of the excitement of my training years was unrelated to medical challenges though. My hospital was a regional center and involved with the concept of developing a newborn transport system in which a team of doctors from our facility would drive to outlying hospitals to begin the treatment of severely ill babies who we'd then transport to our hospital's intensive care unit. This is routinely done now with normal ambulances but we didn't have that luxury back then so our transport experiment was done with a retired bread truck converted into a specially equipped newborn ambulance. It had the latest in incubators, resuscitators, and oxygenators but what it didn't have was seat belts or shock absorbers. Loaves of bread undoubtedly never object to curves or potholes and the infant in the incubator did have a smooth ride but the rest of us riding in back had a ride like a roller coaster. As our driver roared down the highways, running red lights and crossing median strips, we would crash into the walls and throw up hoping that the baby would continue breathing during the times we had to leave his side to lean over a bucket.

Residency years were similar to internship but with increased responsibilities. Having survived the rigors of internship we had greatly increased confidence and with the confidence came increased assertiveness. Over my years as a private practitioner myself I developed sympathy for the primary physicians who had had to deal with us cocky trainees but back then I had no awareness of the difficulties of outpatient care and was insensitive to the necessities of treating families as well as patients.

I recall one private physician who probably out of frustration from his frequent calls had admitted a child very late at night with a mild viral illness. I'm sure that he knew as well as we did that the child was only mildly ill and could have been cared for at home but due to the multiple frantic calls he was getting from the anxious parents he also knew that he wouldn't get any sleep with the child at home and so had admitted her into the hospital. This meant that he could now go back to sleep but it also meant that we had to get up and stay awake the rest of the night in order to examine the child, draw blood, evaluate the results, and talk frequently with the parents. Determined to ensure that the private doctor would enjoy the same lack of sleep that he had arranged for us, we proceeded to call him every two hours all night long to report that the child was doing well, that she was still stable with minimal complaints, or that she was sleeping comfortably, and finally that she was now awake and wanting breakfast.

Interns usually received the first call when there were problems on the ward but the resident had ultimate responsibility. On call duties have improved over the years but when I was a resident interns were on duty every other night often receiving little or no sleep. From a resident's vantage point it was very worrisome to see how readily judgment could be clouded by fatigue.

Early one morning I received a call from the night nurse in intensive care that a girl who had recently had cardiac surgery had suddenly complained of dizziness and had dropped her blood pressure twenty points. My intern had been called and hearing the story while still being half sleep he had sleepily mumbled "I'm not concerned" and fallen back asleep. Rightfully still worried about possible internal bleeding, the nurses had called me to notify me of the situation and the intern's response. As I rushed to examine the patient, I decided that the only justification for my intern's lack of concern was the fact that it had not been his blood pressure that had dropped.

One very troubling realization of residency was the fact that much of medicine's magic was by that time already known to you and that despite dedicated care there were often concrete limits to what doctors could do. When the house staff was unable to swiftly diagnose and cure a patient they usually held on to the hope of being able to get help from the senior attending physicians. This belief was shattered the day I admitted a critically ill little boy who continued to steadily deteriorate despite all of our attempts at therapies. In desperation I called the attending doctor thinking that with his years of experience he would know of some helpful untried strategy to cure the child. I wasted many precious moments on the phone as I detailed the history, lab tests, and therapies we were using and hopefully kept waiting for the attending physician to interrupt with a cataclysmic revelation of some curative procedure. My heart fell when after my long dissertation, the attending's only response was "how sad."

Another recollection was the night when I was on duty at a large city hospital and received a call from the emergency room about a child being admitted to pediatrics via x-ray. Knowing that the child was currently stable and that there was often a back up in X-ray, my intern and I left word to be called as soon as the child finished in x-ray and arrived on the pediatric floor. We then fell back asleep. At rounds the following morning we wondered if we had both had similar dreams about an admission since we had never been called again and no such child was on the floor. It all seemed very odd until the mystery was solved later that morning, four hours after our original call, when the child turned up at pediatrics with a very flustered and embarrassed aide who had apparently gotten lost without a cell phone in the hospital's maze of a basement and had been frantically wheeling the patient's stretcher up and down deserted corridors all night long.

Doctors with Children
and Horses Need Not Apply

A NUMBER OF UNIQUE SITUATIONS arose during internship and residency due to my being a mother as well as a physician. One memorable problem actually started even before internship. Before working in the hospital as an intern I of course had to interview and be offered the position. My husband was going to be working in Bethesda, MD so I knew I needed my position to be at a hospital near there and so interviewed at several in the area.

The interviews were all interesting but my most memorable one was the one at the nearby pediatric hospital. As often happened when arriving in an unfamiliar city I was unable to find a babysitter and so wound up having to take my then 6 month old baby with me for the interview. He was being nursed most of the time but would use a bottle when outside the house so I had brought one with me. The bottles I had were terrific in that they had straws inside that went all the way from inside the nipple straight to the bottom of the bottle so that babies could drink even while sitting up. Those bottles had a big disadvantage however that was totally unknown to me until that interview at the pediatric hospital which was that any squeezing of the nipple would result in milk squirting out as if from a water pistol. I had somehow been totally unaware of this possibility but my son discovered it quickly and spent the entire time of my interview happily squeezing the nipple and spraying milk all across the room. Fortunately my interviewer was a kind understanding pediatrician with a good sense of humor so despite his having been squirted with milk, I did get hired as an intern and resident anyway.

Babysitter problems also occurred later during my residency. I recall one day when my usual babysitter was ill and I couldn't find another on short notice so wound up having to take my then 3 year old son with me to the hospital. I settled him down with crayons and coloring book at the nurses' station while I dealt with the patients but then had him accompany me on rounds with the attending physician since at that time we'd be discussing cases in the corridors and not interfacing with any patients who were sick. Attending rounds were supposed to only take an hour since as housestaff we had so many other time consuming responsibilities and so many sick patients to care for but the particular attending that month loved to hear himself talk and would happily drone on for two or more hours with none of us ever courageous enough to interrupt.

I loved being with my son but having him with me in the hospital all day and my having to constantly keep flipping back and forth between my mother and doctor roles was very stressful. It did turn out to have an unforeseen huge benefit though and in fact he became a housestaff hero when, as the attending physician giving rounds went on and on into his second hour of trivial chit chat, my son suddenly tugged on my skirt and whispered loudly enough for everyone to hear, "Mommy, when will that man stop talking so we can have lunch?" The attending promptly checked his watch, apologized and ended his talk while the rest of the housestaff hugged my son and pleaded with me to bring him every day.

Other unique situations unrelated to medical care or to parenthood also arose during my housestaff days by the fact of my being a physician who also had animals. We lived in a rural area about an hour from the hospital and right after buying the house I had started fulfilling all my childhood dreams by accumulating many pets including a backyard horse. One cold winter night when I was on duty at the hospital I received a frantic call from home that my horse had escaped the corral and couldn't be found. My fellow housestaff seemed pretty skeptical but grudgingly obliged when I asked them to take over my patients' care for an hour or two while I left the hospital and raced home with a flashlight to try to follow hoofprints through the snowy woods.

To Pee or Not to Pee

FINALLY I WAS DONE with my training and confidently joined a private practice in the town where we lived. I expected things there to be fairly routine and much less intense than in the hospital but that wasn't the case. Many common parts of the physical exam become unusual when dealing with children and many simple office procedures I had learned became challenging. To examine a fearful toddler, I often had to examine mommy's throat, big brother's throat, and even teddy bear's throat.

I felt children's bellies looking for Cheerios and peanut butter, I hunted in ears for hiding puppies and listened to chests while imaginary birthday candles were blown out. I examined children on the office table, on their mothers' laps, on the floor and with both of us hiding behind a chair. I was hugged, kissed, bitten, and kicked accepting all with equanimity but one of the more difficult tasks turned out to be the seemingly easy one of obtaining a urine sample.

To begin with, teenagers do not like to admit to any bodily functions. The idea of peeing on command into a cup and showing it to anyone is considered definitely gross and many claimed to be unable to void at all. Toddlers also seemed to lose the ability to pee on command as soon as they entered the office. Mothers would go into the bathroom with their toddler and plead sweetly or demand angrily with equally negative result. The nurse would run the water in the sink and the child would drink cup after cup of water to no avail. Through the bathroom door I once even heard one child ask his mother if she couldn't please help him by going in the cup herself and telling the nurse that he had done it. One four year old however went into the bathroom happily after being told how to give a urine sample only to come out after a few minutes stating sadly that it might be broken because, "It won't work."

The secret to success seemed to lie elsewhere though because invariably, as soon as the waterlogged child was bundled back into his snowsuit, strapped into his car seat, and on the highway home, he would need to immediately find a bathroom.

On one occasion a small child went into the office bathroom alone, urine sample cup in hand. She emerged a short while later with a damp cup triumphantly saying she had finally done it. She had urinated in the cup and then somehow thinking that that was all we had wanted, she had dumped the urine into the toilet and flushed it, carrying back to us the now wet but empty cup.

One enterprising young boy gave a urine sample in the cup and found it such an entertaining experience that at home he apparently went into a phase of only peeing in cups. Each morning for two weeks after his office exam his parents would find gifts of little paper cups of urine all lined up on the bathroom sink

After being asked to pee in the cup, some three year olds would just look at me incredulously as if I'd lost my mind. They would then state emphatically that, "Big boys pee in potties not in cups." Although I always try to explain to children why we need them to pee in the cup, there obviously remains much confusion as to why we're so interested in their urine and whether or not our toilets function normally. One day I was examining a baby and noticed her four year old brother looking very uncomfortable. When I asked him what was wrong, he said that he had to go "potty." I assured him that he could use our office toilet but saw him continue to hesitate as he explained that he actually had to do a "doody." I reassured him that that was fine and that he could still use our toilet. He still stood there hesitantly and then fearfully asked if he had to do it in a cup.

Another challenging part of examining children is getting them dressed and undressed. Many a young child will be unwilling to part with his Smurf shirt prior to being examined, yet once undressed will delight in parading about the entire office and waiting area stark naked. Some toddlers after being done with their exam and fully dressed to go back home would diligently peel off their shoes and socks while their mother was distracted talking to me. They'd then remove the rest of their clothes, explore the office trash can for abandoned treasures, and finally escape, totally nude, into the hall, peering into other examining rooms and generally refusing to get redressed again.

Teenagers are more modest. On occasion some of them would be unwilling to get undressed at all. One determined teenager had to be weighed fully dressed including a belted winter coat. She did tentatively allow one arm out for a blood pressure reading but finally had to have the rest of her exam rescheduled for another day when she said she might be less nervous.

One teenage girl was even more determined. She very cooperatively got into the examining gown and went to the bathroom to give a urine sample but then somehow escaped through the bathroom window leaving her clothes in the exam room, the mystified nurse outside the door and her totally baffled mother still sitting in the waiting room.

Generally though my patients loved coming to the office and no matter how hectic my day I never rushed people and so parents always felt that their child was very special to me. This actually was true but did lead some parents to feel that I would always fit them in to be seen on a moment's notice the same day they called no matter how trivial their concern and no matter how booked my day and they would get furious with the staff if ever told I couldn't. This became especially clear one morning after a night during which I had suddenly had to be rushed to the hospital needing emergency surgery.

When in the morning my office called my patients who had scheduled routine visits for that day to tell them that I had just had emergency surgery and so their appointments would have to rescheduled, most parents expressed concern about me and were very understanding. One mother however became irate saying that she had scheduled her child's visit months before and didn't want to reschedule. Even after being told again that I was in the hospital having just had unexpected emergency surgery she remained mad and didn't see the craziness of her complaint and calm down until after my partner took the phone and told her that he was sure I would want to accommodate her so if she took her child to the hospital where I had just had my surgery, he was sure I'd be happy to do the child's physical exam in the recovery room just as soon as I was awake from the anesthesia.

In One Ear and Out the Other

BEING IN PRACTICE FOR so many years gave me an inside look at many families and the complex interactions among the people in them. Many times I'd watch siblings peer into their infant brothers left ear to see if the otoscope light I was using in the right ear would shine through and I'd meditate on the wonder of imagination and the human brain.

From decades of observing parents I came to the belief that part of a mother's intelligence often goes to her developing baby while she's pregnant. I certainly feel as if this happened with me since I seemed to become increasingly forgetful with each pregnancy. Highly educated women after delivery seemed to adopt a new way of thinking and often a new form of speech in which they'd find themselves reflexively pointing out choo choos and doggies to their adult friends just the way they did with their children. They would also call their pediatricians with questions which would have amazed them before they had had a child.

An example is the mother who perfectly seriously called the office with the question of whether it would be alright for her two year old to snack on cat chow while watching cartoons on TV.

Another mother was being driven to distraction by her school age child's frequent complaints of headaches. After taking a careful history and doing a full exam I determined that the headaches were most likely due to pressures her son was feeling. She was reassured by the diagnosis but called the office the next day with the question of whether I felt that giving the child a haircut would help by lessening the pressure. Another otherwise highly intelligent mother brought her baby in smelling like a garbage pail. As I undressed the baby I discovered the reason for the odor. She had heard that starch can help diaper rashes and so had filled the baby's diaper with old potato peelings.

It is easy to keep a straight face when parents ask seemingly foolish questions though when I think about how ignorant I must sound at the car repair shop. Some parents' remarks, however, do deserve mention for being harder than others to ignore. One is the answer of the parent who was asked whether her child had Medicaid. She responded, "No, I think he's got bronchitis."

Parents would sometimes bring in a child totally covered from head to foot with red spots which I would diagnose to be an allergic reaction to a new food. On hearing that the rash was an allergy, many parents would then look with delight at their red, blotchy, unhappily itchy child and say, "Oh, I'm so glad, I was afraid that he might have developed a rash."

We all make remarks with an occasional wrong word but one of our nurses did it more often than most. When infants had a bad runny nose, we often advised their mothers to use salt water nose drops (one brand name being called "Ocean") and then suction out the baby's nose with a rubber bulb aspirator. One day I overheard our harried nurse tell a new mother on the phone to help the baby's cold by giving him "Ocean Spray" and then using a plunger. I was able to quickly correct this statement to the mother before she fed her baby cranberry juice and plunked the toilet plunger over his face.

Parents often use wrong words too and sometimes the use of a wrong word can be very telling. Once late at night a mother who had been impatiently suctioning her baby's nose all evening called me to complain that her child still had a cold even though she'd been "exasperating" his nose every hour.

One of our most popular nurses was in fact a superb nurse but did have the distinction of using the most unusual words or having the most odd occurrences. Once she called out a new patient's name in the waiting room. The very youthful looking father got up from his seat and followed her into the exam room while the mother, unnoticed by the nurse, was still collecting her things together in order to bring the baby. Seeing no one else in the examining room, the nurse assumed that the young man who had followed her was the patient and so to his astonishment she calmly told him to take off all his clothes and hop up onto the examining table. The family was new to the office and I'm sure a bit shocked by what the father must have thought was our very strange way of getting to know people.

Another time that same nurse was alone in the office on a Saturday morning. As she was walking through the waiting room on her way to the rest room the mailman arrived. He was new to our route and unfamiliar with our office so when he saw her he asked her where he should put the mail. She helpfully told him to follow her as she walked through the waiting room toward the desk in the main part of the office where we kept our mail. Assuming that he had noticed the pile of other mail on the desk, she continued walking past the desk and went on into the ladies room where she turned and found to her astonishment that the mailman had still been following and was now also in the ladies room right behind her with a very puzzled look on his face,

Even when we used the correct words, children often misheard or misunderstood what we were saying. Sometimes this led to unusual conversations. One usually very cooperative 7 year old balked at receiving his yearly TB test. The nurse tried to reassure him and reminded him that he had had that test many times before and asked why he didn't want the TB test this year. He looked about to cry and stammered that if he took it, his mother would then know how much T.V. he watched. Another time I was examining a teenage girl and with my stethoscope on her chest to listen to her lungs I asked her to take some nice big breaths. She froze and gave me an angry look as she demanded to know why I was commenting on her nice big "breasts." Another day, a 6 year old who was usually quite frightened by the possibility of getting any shots, became upset instead of reassured when I told him that the nurse wouldn't have to be giving him any "pokes" that day. When I looked puzzled as to why he was upset about that, he explained that he was really very thirsty and would have really liked to have had the "Coke."

A BALANCE OF SANITY

MEDICINE TURNED OUT TO be a much more demanding career than I had anticipated but it also had many rewards, some of which were totally unexpected. One of these was the time my husband brought home a pet turtle. I had learned that turtles often carry the contagious salmonella germ but rather than blindly bringing the turtle back to the store and possibly disappointing my son for no reason, I decided to place the turtle in quarantine at our house while asking one of the hospital lab technicians to do me a favor and test a sample of the turtle's water. Being honest, though unimaginative, I labeled the sample "turtle water."

My hospital at the time was in a section of Washington, D.C. where many families had unusual names and as the lab technician who had agreed to test the sample began processing it he paused to ask casually what type of specimen this was of "Turtlewater's", to which I replied again that it was simply "turtle water." He tried to clarify his question by asking more precisely whether the sample was urine or was it stool?

To that query I gave up on just repeating that it was turtle water and simply stated that since it was "turtle water" it was therefore probably urine and stool both. At that he stared at me for a while before changing tactics and asking with evident frustration whether other doctors were involved in the case who might know what type specimen it was or whether Turtlewater was a private patient of mine.

Eventually he understood and we were able to determine that the turtle water did in fact contain salmonella bacteria. Being unable to learn how to treat this in a small turtle or even whether to count the weight of the animal's shell in calculating medication dosages, we reluctantly returned the turtle.

It had helped being a physician in the case of the turtle but most days it was hard juggling the demands of medicine and my family. This schizophrenic existence was described best by a small patient of mine who, in confusion, used to call me the combination name of "Mrs. Pepperdoctorcorn", a label I still love to this day. On the other hand being a parent myself made it very easy to identify with the parents and families I dealt with. This was very helpful in knowing how best to handle the emotions they were facing when their child was injured or ill but it did give me the disturbing distinction of being one of the few doctors who cried along with the family when a patient died.

Medicine can clearly be challenging and caring for extremely sick patients often very stressful but I was usually able to maintain a balance of sanity in handling life and death crises by the natural humor inherent in dealing with children. I remember listening to a youngster's heart and lungs at the necessary different chest locations and suddenly noticing his frightened face as he asked whether I was listening at so many places because his heart couldn't be found.

Another time a small girl who I had let listen through my stethoscope to her own heart had a similar terrified look come over her face as she urgently whispered to me that she couldn't hear her "beeps" and thought she might be dead.

The most bizarre interactions, however, were with parents who at times of stress from worrying about their child's possible illnesses often seemed to lose all common sense. One mother brought her son to the DC emergency room at midnight through a ghetto riot and past police barricades to see why his hair had been thinning out over the past several weeks only to discover at the hospital that he had been pulling it out himself. Not having known that in advance did make it a reasonable concern but it seemed to me he was at a greater risk of losing his entire head by coming in at that time of night through a riot. Another time a father called in the middle of the night because his child was having severe diarrhea. The only non water liquid in the house was Jell-O so he was advised to give the child Jell-O water to drink. He called back an hour later asking which was better to use, the large or small package of Jell-O. He was told that it really didn't matter. When he insisted on an answer, however, he was finally told that probably the large package would be better. This allowed him to snarl, "I told you so," to his wife as he reported that all they had at home was the small packages. There were also parents who arrived at the office in tears extremely concerned about their child's terrible rash which had suddenly appeared that afternoon but which in our office turned out to just be from magic markers and easily washed away.

Although I did occasionally make house calls, most physicians never did and those I made were very few and far between. This led to many typically frustrating conversations. One example was the early Sunday morning when a mother woke my partner at 5 am to tell him that her child had a terrible earache. He advised her to give some household pain medication and that he'd see her child in the office first thing at 9:00. She became furious saying she couldn't wait until 9:00 because her child had been crying for an hour already. He responded that if she wanted he could go and meet her at the office right away. To this offer she bellowed with even more incredulous anger that she couldn't possibly wake her husband at that hour to drive her to the office, didn't my partner realize what time it was, and that it was only 5 o'clock in the morning!

A further frustrating night time recollection was the 3:00 am call I once got about a two year old child who couldn't sleep and was terribly hoarse. Before I could ask any other questions or in fact say anything at all the mother said she was putting her son on the phone so I could hear his voice. My husband lay there wide-eyed with the phone cord stretched across his throat to my side of the bed during my ensuing half hour conversation with a very bright and very verbal toddler who was clearly not too sick and refused all my requests, demands, and pleadings that he hand the phone back to his mother.

On another occasion a parent made an urgent middle of the night call with worries about her child's severe stomachache, headache, sore throat, and high fever. After being told how to make her child comfortable for the rest of the night and that I would see him first thing in the morning, the mother then asked if it would possibly be all right to bring him to the office in the afternoon instead because he was supposed to be in a swim meet that morning.

That incident contrasts with that of the teenager who hated art class in school but loved gym. He came into the office one day with a sprained ankle and a plaintive plea for me to let him play in his next day's soccer game but to please give him a written excuse from art class due to his injured leg.

As more and more of these types of interactions occurred it began to seem that having a child must take away all one's common sense as otherwise highly intelligent parents would often get overwhelmed by the very fact of having a child and say or do odd out of character strange things.

As an example I still recall with amazement a friend who raved about the fantastic pediatrician she had had at the Boston Hospital where she had just delivered her first baby. She had been especially impressed by his thoroughness in including a long talk on taking the baby home for the first time and carefully introducing her to the family dog. He had apparently detailed at length how to let the dog sniff the new baby while the parents supervised and before ever being left alone with the baby to be sure the dog had learned that the baby was part of the family. When my friend finished relating this tale, I had to agree that the pediatrician did sound wonderful and extremely thorough and thoughtful but wondered why she had found this so helpful since the fact was that she actually did not own a dog and so would have to borrow mine.

Another time a friend came home from the hospital after having delivered her first baby. In the hospital she had taken all the new mother classes on the proper way to burp, diaper and bathe a baby but had just come home and was still anxious so after work I decided to stop by her house and see how she was doing. I arrived just as she was finishing the baby's first bath. She was holding her naked, dripping wet, screaming infant in the air as I came in and had turned with relief on seeing me and asked me to remind her what it was she was supposed to do next. Having a baby had wiped away all her common sense memories of getting out of a shower dripping wet and grabbing a towel.

On the other side of the coin though were the parents who were way too casual about their children's illnesses. One morning a mother called to tell me that her son smelled funny and was vomiting and lethargic but when told to bring him in right away she hesitated and said that he had just fallen asleep so she thought she'd maybe give him 4-5 hours to rest and let me know later that night how he was doing. From the symptoms she was describing I was extremely concerned though so insisted she wake him up and come in right away. Fortunately I prevailed because when she brought him in I saw that he was practically comatose with what turned out to be ketoacidosis from new onset diabetes and after being quickly stabilized in the office, needed to go by ambulance directly to the hospital.

Lack of sleep at night and crying babies during the day can affect doctors and nurses as well as parents though and with our large practice it was easy to understand the Freudian slip of our receptionist as she answered one of our three constantly-ringing phones on a particularly busy day with the plaintive, "Pediatric Associates, can you help me?"

All the stresses and nocturnal awakenings seemed worthwhile, however, on the occasions like the one when a little girl who had recovered from a severe case of bronchitis popped into the office to give me a picture she had drawn for me and to tell me that she had decided to grow up into a hugging doctor like me.

Where Have All the Sitters Gone

A MAJOR PROBLEM OF BEING a mother and a physician was of course the need for reliable baby sitters and household help. The search became an endless quest because it was very hard to leave our infant with a stranger altogether and finding someone we could totally trust proved even harder. The required hours were also hard for the sitter. Sitters had to arrive by 7:30 so I could make hospital rounds before going to the office and had to stay variable lengths of time depending on whether or not any emergencies had arisen at the end of the day.

We had one sitter in Washington, D.C. who was marvelous. She was a retired school teacher who came to our house armed with lesson plans, scheduled activities and projects. She usually came at least a half hour earlier than we expected her so that she could prepare her supplies, cutouts or puppets for the day. She was warm, loving, bright and energetic. Our son was only two at the time but this woman had him charting weather, painting murals, and loving to play with numbers and letters. Unfortunately, we had to move from the area and she couldn't come with us. That lady's worst fault was that she spoiled us. We were totally unprepared for the ensuing chain of soap opera addicts who cared for our child in Massachusetts.

When we first returned to Boston, we decided to try live-in help since my husband and I would occasionally both be on duty the same night. The first woman turned out to be a chain smoker and even though she claimed to only smoke with her head hanging out the window, we had to let her go along with all the blankets and pillows from her room that still reeked of smoke. The next woman was very sweet but had to leave after just two months due to problems in her own family. With my husband and I both working full time it was hard finding time to interview sitter candidates but we tried once again.

The first applicant was a stunning young girl with long strawberry blond hair from Ireland. She was anxious to have the job having just arrived in the US the week before but had no experience at all with children. She seemed sweet but had no references other than friends, had had no prior babysitting experience, and had been the youngest in her family so hadn't even had the experience of caring for her siblings. Despite that total lack of experience my husband said he thought she'd be perfect. I suspect his decision was based on the long length of her hair and short length of her skirt but needless to say I didn't hire her.

The final woman we interviewed was a loving grandmother-type lady and we immediately warmed to her and gave her the job. She moved in right away and as we had anticipated she cuddled and bundled the children tirelessly. She was also a good cook so we felt very lucky to have found her. I did however personally find her a bit difficult to deal with because she was of the generation of women who worshiped men and so in addition to caring for our children she waited on my husband hand and foot. If he was delayed at the hospital she stalled dinner until the children and I were ready to eat the chairs and waited to announce that everything was finally ready until the sound of my husband's key was in the lock when she'd magically declare the meal was done cooking.

On the other hand, when I was delayed at the hospital, I would arrive home not only after everyone had eaten but after the last crumbs had been wrapped up and refrigerated to a tasty coldness. The sitter would apologetically say that she had had to feed the rest of the family first because she knew how hungry men can get if they have to wait.

Live in help was necessary since we needed someone at the house in case we both got called out in the middle of the night at the same time but having that degree of security did have several drawbacks. The biggest problem we discovered was that the sitter's daily concerns became our daily concerns as well. The grandmotherly live in sitter we had hired had a car which was old and beyond repair with a battery that was terminal. I actually often wondered why she bothered to have a battery in her car at all since whenever she wanted to go anyplace I had to jump start her car from my car's battery. This event occurred at least once a week and occasionally more often so I must have done it scores of times but each time I did it she would ask if I was sure I knew how or whether we should wait for "my man" to come home.

The one time she did wait for my man to come was a snowy night when my husband and I had theater tickets. Just as we were all dressed and ready to leave she announced that she had arranged for another lady to watch the children briefly since she had decided to go out for a while herself. As usual though, she stated that she was unable to start or move her car. After starting her motor in our usual jump start fashion and worriedly watching the minutes pass, we proceeded to unsuccessfully try again and again to manually push her car out of the snow and ice. As we huffed and puffed behind her car and became later and later for our show she repeatedly gunned her motor, spun her wheels, and splashed snow, mud, and sand all over the front of our clothes. She finally got out of the car in despair and asked if maybe one of us could try driving the car. I got into her car prepared to gun the motor like she had only to discover that the whole time she had been unable to move her car while we had been pushing, she had had the emergency brake on. Once the brake was released the car sailed easily up the drive leaving us exhausted, covered in mud, and late for our show.

Despite the aggravations she caused me, our children loved her and my husband enjoyed her attentions so she remained part of our household for several years. When she finally retired and left our family, my sons refused to allow another sitter in the house. A parade of ladies came, said, "What adorable boys," and left after their first day because the boys had behaved badly and told them that they hated them.

In the middle of a particularly busy day at the office one frantic new sitter called to tell me that my son wouldn't go near her or talk to her. I advised her to sit down and read a children's book out loud and that since he loved books he'd soon come over. She called me back shortly to say that he had heard her reading but instead of coming over he was crying and telling her to stay in the other room because he didn't want to hear her voice or see her face. My heart broke but I couldn't tell the children at the office to come back later with their wheezing attacks, earaches and fractured fingers. That was one of many many days that I wished I could be at least two people so I could be both at home and in the office all at the same time.

Broiled Whatever It Was

THE DEMANDS OF PRIVATE practice were great but equally challenging were the demands of being a housewife and the need to try to produce nutritious meals each night. I am convinced that one of the things that helped my husband decide that he could accept my being a working wife was the arrival of my first pay check along with the realization that I was not and could not ever be a cook as fabulous as his mother was even if he chained me to the stove for a year.

While trying to study anatomy and pharmacology in medical school, I had also tried to learn how to cook. It was fortunate that we didn't starve since my aptitude for medical skills proved much greater than that for culinary skills. The first startling dish I made was chili con carne with a recipe which must have come straight from a fire-eating Mexican. I absentmindedly kept adding chili powder as directed without tasting what I was making until after it was done. To call that chili "hot" was an understatement. There was nothing else to eat in the house so in order to be able to eventually eat dinner that night we had to put the chili in a strainer under the faucet and wash off all the sauce.

Next my husband tried his hand at cooking and attempted French onion soup. After dirtying every pot, pan, and utensil in the house he finally put his masterpiece in the oven and anxiously sat and waited for the soup to cook. When the time was up and we finally took it out of the oven we realized that all the soup had evaporated and what we had left was elegant little bowls with cheese topped soggy bread at the bottom.

We had to improve soon since we had invited company for dinner the following week.

The night of the dinner party came and I studied the cook book and carefully prepared a fancy dinner of lobster bisque soup and beef stroganoff. The meal was memorable. At the last second I realized that I had made a mistake with the recipe and that there wouldn't be enough lobster bisque for everyone so, picking a can of similarly colored soup so that no one would notice, I gave my husband and myself tomato rice soup. My second mistake was not telling my husband about this in advance. As the guests raved about the lobster in the soup my husband announced to everyone that something was odd because his soup had no lobster and just had rice.

What was even worse, though, was the beef stroganoff because, being preoccupied with worries about a very sick patient at the hospital, I had totally forgotten to add the characteristic sour cream to the beef sauce. This time all the guests could wonder together what in fact it was that they were eating.

As time went by things from the kitchen got no better. The night of another dinner party I miscalculated in making the recipes for our company so that every drop of dinner had been dispensed with in the very first serving. I sat mutely as my husband glared at what he thought was my apparent lack of manners and asked our guests if they'd like second helpings. I breathed a sigh of relief as they all said no until I heard my husband insist that they should all please ask for seconds or that I would be insulted. When eventually one guest said he'd been persuaded to have another helping, I had to smile sweetly and say that actually there was no more.

The next time I tried what I thought would be an easier approach to a dinner party. I decided to have little rock Cornish hens, one per guest. What I never realized was that those little hens expand and grow in the oven so that when the time came to serve dinner that night each person had on their plate what looked like their own individual family-size roast chicken with no room to put any of the fancy vegetables or salads that I had slaved over. Of course, even that night with the hens can't compare to the disastrous time when I put an entire frozen chicken on the counter to thaw in time to make it for dinner, dashed to the store, and returned an hour later to find no sign at all of the chicken. I was dismayed and decided that I must have forgotten to take the chicken out of the freezer altogether until the mystery was solved when I discovered my dog under the bed with the remains of a cellophane wrapper and a huge smile. It actually seemed only fair that she had eaten our chicken though since several weeks earlier a hungry teenager visiting the house had raided the ice box and thinking he had discovered hash, had devoured a dish of the dog's food.

Somehow my husband and I both did learn to cook though and make often requested lasagna, spaghetti, and snack pizzas as well as heirloom chicken and pot roast recipes. However, I have never turned on the oven without recalling our most famous meal of all, the broiled whatever-it-was in Maryland. That night I had come home late from work, had put our baby to bed, and was in a bathrobe casually broiling a steak. I suddenly noticed that the fat had set the oven on fire and being unable to recall which white household powder puts out oven fires I threw them all; salt, baking powder, baking soda, flour, everything. I made a complete mess and the oven fire kept burning quietly but persistently.

In desperation I called the fire department and asked them to please send over a man with a fire extinguisher because there was a small fire in my oven that was all self-contained but wouldn't go out. I assured them that nothing else was burning so all that was needed was a small fire extinguisher. I sat waiting for the lone fireman to come while listening to distant sirens and bells and wondering where there was a fire of such magnitude. Suddenly, I realized that all the commotion had stopped after arriving at my house as two hook and ladders, a chief's car, ambulance, and police car all roared up.

My husband disappeared outside to gawk with the neighbors as a dozen suited and helmeted firemen stormed into the house, hatchets in hand, to find the fire. When they reached the kitchen and started to fan out the smoke they peered at the now-sizzled dinner in the oven and stood around laughing while trying to guess what it had been that I had been cooking.

All these cooking traumas finally did end though partially because I did finally learn how to cook and also because I wound up becoming vegetarian so there was no longer any issue of burnt steak or exploding chicken.

This decision to become vegetarian had come to me late in my career and my partners were dead set against my discussing it with any of my patients but it did come up once on its own when a mother asked me to please tell her daughter that in order to grow strong she had to eat her meat. I knew from my research that that wasn't true but also knew that my partners would be upset if I didn't follow the usual party line nutritional advice of our office. While I was debating with myself what to tell the woman's daughter, the little girl looked up at me with her big soulful eyes and sadly said, "But I just can't eat anything that ever had a face."

That did it for me, I told the mother that actually her daughter had a good point and that I agreed with her so couldn't tell her to eat her meat. I also told the mother that if my not doing that was upsetting to her then she had the option of switching her daughter's care to one of my partners. The mother stared at me for a while and then quietly asked if I could help teach her how to prepare healthy vegetarian meals. Her daughter remained my patient and did grow into a lovely strong woman without eating any meat and the vision of her telling me she couldn't eat anything with a face remained with me too and over the years bolstered my resolve whenever I wavered.

STRANGERS DOING THE HOUSEWORK

MEALTIMES WEREN'T THE ONLY challenge of being a wife in the 60's and 70's. I often think that I was one of the first truly liberated women. My family never questioned my freedom to simultaneously work full time at a career and to work full time at home. It was, therefore, quite a revelation to discover that it was possible to hire someone to help with the children and the housework so that I could go to work without a companion infant on my hip and could read without balancing the book on the pile of wash I was folding. Somehow, however, just like the problem trying to find good sitters, the devoted jewels of mother's helpers all eluded me.

My first attempt at hiring a cleaning lady was through an agency. They sent a lovely, earnest woman who promised to thoroughly clean the house in a single afternoon. I knew this was an impossible task in my household of children, dogs, cats and rabbits but was nonetheless astonished when after four hours she was still engrossed in cleaning the same bedroom she had started in. I knew my son's room reflected the tastes and collections of an all-American boy but since I couldn't imagine it taking that long to scour even the horse stalls, I decided she had to leave.

Next I hired a cleaning service who promised a spic and span home with a minimum and guaranteed four hour stay. What could I lose? My son's room had to already be spotlessly clean. The man from the agency who arrived at my house seemed honest and hardworking and I guess I shouldn't blame him that almost as soon as he arrived there was a total power failure on my street. I'm sure he would have vacuumed if the vacuum ran on batteries and I'm sure he would have dusted if there had been enough light to see the dust. Instead, however, he commiserated on the vulnerability of above ground electrical wires, played chess with my son, and collected his money for having spent a pleasant four hour's visit with us.

This left me pretty discouraged and it wasn't until we could play tic tac toe with our fingers on the coffee table dust that I decided to try again. This time I relied on the advice of friends. The first friend I asked recommended her cleaning lady of many years duration. I therefore happily hired Janet and promptly found myself paying by the hour as this new cleaning lady spent her time relating long tales of woe including all her past illnesses and husband troubles while generally ignoring the dust and the wash.

Two weeks after I had hired Janet, my friend who had recommended her called to tell me that the lady's work had deteriorated and that she had fired her. This was a near disaster since I am incapable of firing anyone and was especially so after hearing as many stories of personal hardship as Janet continued to tell me. I had almost resorted to hiring another cleaning lady to come clean before or after Janet came, when to my delight she decided to change careers and give up cleaning altogether. This was probably less of a surprise to me than to her family since I knew she had obviously given up housecleaning a long time ago.

I decided to try one more time but my luck seemed to be consistent since the first applicant for the job, right after saying hello, stated in no uncertain terms that she actually didn't really like doing housework, was not meticulous, and could not abide being told what to do. I was so intimidated by her manner though that had she insisted I would have hired her at once. She was not hired, however, since with my husband's coaching I was able to use the ruse of cowardly housewives and state that although I really liked her, my husband had changed his mind and decided that he didn't want strangers doing the housework. Thus it was that my lie became true and I continued to be liberated to work all day at the office and again all evening at home.

HOUSECALLS

IN ADDITION TO THE challenges of finding good household help for inside the house, there were also problems with the house itself that added to the chaos of managing a home and an office. The house we lived in was fairly young when we bought it but like all houses it always seemed to need constant attention to keep it happy and sturdy. My husband tried to help but was actually no more skilled at repair work than my brother-in-law who one day carefully turned over his dining room table to re-nail its legs only to discover that when finished he had nailed the table securely upside down to the floor.

It once took my husband an entire day to replace our front door spring closure. Afterward he showed it to all guests as proudly as a work of art. The first sign of trouble though came with the first windy day when the door flew open, smacked the side of the house and shattered its glass window. I didn't say anything as I vacuumed slivers of glass from the shrubs and he readjusted the spring. All was then well until the next windy day when once more the door flew open, smacked the side of the house and shattered its new glass window. This time I was smarter and replaced the window with unbreakable hard plastic as my husband readjusted the spring a second time.

Sure enough, there was soon another windy day and once again the door flew open and smacked the side of the house. This time the heavy plastic window stayed intact but this time the door frame itself shattered into a true jigsaw puzzle of splinters and broken pieces of door.

My husband decided at that point to hire a handyman. The first handyman did correctly fix the door and then agreed to hang new wallpaper for us in our downstairs hall. Two days before my entire family was arriving for a Thanksgiving weekend the wallpaper arrived as did the handyman. He busily stripped off the old paper, set up ladders and buckets all over the place and sloshed glue around for about two hours. At that point he folded his ladders, looked sadly at the half-covered peeling walls and announced that he guessed he was no longer able to remember how to hang paper so he was going home. I was ready to hang him but figured that since my in-laws had not objected on a prior visit when the septic system had suddenly backed up and they had been asked to pee outside behind a tree, they would hopefully not be bothered by the bomb shelter appearance of the walls.

That earlier mentioned repair of our septic system had been a near disaster of its own. The excavating company that installed septic systems had tried to dig a new leaching field on our side lawn but instead treated us to a close-up of the Old Faithful geyser as they accidentally hit the main waterline to the house. The only remaining area to dig a leaching field was our front lawn, my husband's "look but don't step" pride and joy. We obviously couldn't dig up a neighbor's yard and we didn't feel right about filling in all the holes and quickly selling the house before flushing any more toilets, so the front lawn wound up having to go.

After that the house generally held together for quite a while until we began noticing that the chimney was standing apart from the house. A mason was called and gave the opinion that the chimney was falling away. He gave an estimate on a repair job which would entail totally taking down the current chimney and then completely rebuilding it while strapping it securely to the house. Fortunately, we obtained a second opinion. This mason measured more precisely and determined definitively that the chimney was absolutely straight and that it was the house that had been sinking. Since it did seem ludicrous to try to hold up a house by tying it to a chimney we did nothing and returned to watching for cracks in the walls and waiting for the furniture to slide in case the house continued its downward descent.

Our house actually seemed cursed by repairman's skills as well as by inherent flaws in construction. I still remember the winter when our electrician replaced our electric heat thermostats before leaving on a three week vacation. He may have also been secretly working for the electric company since whatever he did to our thermostat resulted in our kitchen and living room roasting at a permanent 90 degrees. As we twisted dials, flipped switches, and sat around in bathing suits looking enviously at the snow outside the open windows and doors we frantically tried unsuccessfully to locate other electricians as we watched our utility bill soar.

It was a different electrician who finally did come and solve the heat problem and while he was here I asked him if he could also maybe check why one burner of our electric stove often gave me shocks. I disliked cooking anyway but to suddenly and randomly get an electric jolt while cooking was bound to result in our family's eventually just eating raw food or starving. As I explained the problem with the stove, the man gave me the condescending look that repairmen often give housewives as he explained how electric stoves use electricity and how some people pick up currents in the air and how maybe I had my finger on a wire while standing in a puddle at the time of my shocks. I listened politely and sweetly and then asked him to please check the burner anyway.

While continuing to talk to me in his "you're too dumb to understand this" attitude, he suddenly let out a yelp and jumped six feet backwards, glowering at the stove which had just given him what measured to be a 10 volt shock. I continued to smile quietly as he disconnected the faulty burner and told me that I was lucky he had come since what he had had discovered was that I had a major current leak in that burner and needed it permanently disconnected. It was just as well. Now we had to have simpler meals using no more than three burners or else had to eat out.

After that the house was finally in fairly good shape with its three burner stove, separated chimney and somewhat peeling wallpaper but I kept waiting for the next disaster as I counted new cracks in the living room walls and heard my son leaping and shooting baskets in his bedroom upstairs. While listening to him I couldn't help wondering who'd you call if your child jumped for a hookshot and on landing came right through the bedroom floor onto the downstairs living room sofa.

Do You See What I See

MEANWHILE THE CHALLENGES AT work continued. My office routinely checked children's vision at each yearly exam starting at age three. The younger children were tested with a vision chart showing pictures of everyday items such as cups, boats, hearts, hands and stars or by a chart showing pictures of hands pointing up, down, or sideways. Our nurse would ask small children to cover one eye and tell her what picture she was pointing to or to show her which direction the hands were pointing by imitating the pictures with his or her own hands depending on which chart was being used. The resulting hilarity would be best shown on videotape but can hopefully be understood from the following examples of typical interchanges.

Most children are happy to play the "eye game" but have no clue as to its purpose. Often I'd see a child try to be helpful even when seeing nothing. For example, one child cooperatively covered his right eye when told and then when asked to cover his left eye, went ahead and covered the left eye without first uncovering the right eye which made both his eyes now covered. The nurse who was looking at the chart instead of at the child got increasingly concerned as the child kept being unable to see anything at all on the chart no matter how large a picture she was pointing to. Suddenly sensing her concern but still with both eyes covered, the little boy then tried randomly guessing the pictures until the nurse finally turned around, saw what was happening and explained that at a least one eye had to be uncovered in order to play the game.

Some children proudly recited in turn, "Cup, heart, star" etc. until the pictures got too small for them to see. At that point they'd often bravely try to keep playing by continuing to enthusiastically call out, "Dot, another dot, a smaller dot." When finding the pictures too small, some other children would uncover both eyes, run right up to the chart to peer at the pictures and then run back to where they had been standing now saying cup or boat or whatever the picture had been.

Some children who are generally unsure of themselves will turn to their mother for help when confronted by the eye chart. As the nurse asks, "What is this?" they turn and ask their mother, "What is it? You tell her what it is." Some creative but easily distracted children try to helpfully continue to call out cup or boat as the nurse points to pictures but while they are meanwhile paying no attention at all to the nurse and are watching another child in a distant room instead of looking at the eye chart.

The part with pictures of hands could also be challenging as children would try to hold their hands in the same position as the picture sometimes twisting their whole body around to try to make their hand turn inward. One child watched carefully as our nurse used her own hand to show how to make your hand look like the hands on the eye chart. However, when it was the child's turn to "make your hand look like this", little girl sadly stated that she couldn't make her hand look like the nurse's because her nails weren't painted red.

Embarrassing moments also sometimes happened in these routine eye exams when the nurse had failed to just look at the patient's chart to discover any history of previous eye disease. One day our nurse was doing the eye chart with an eight year old who had unfortunately had to have one eye surgically removed due to a tumor discovered when he was an infant. He naturally assumed that the nurse knew what she was doing and had good reason to ask when she asked him to cover one eye and read off the letters on the chart. He readily covered his unseeing glass eye and read the letters perfectly with his good eye. The nurse then asked him to switch eyes and read the chart again. Without any protest, he cooperatively covered his good eye and stood facing the chart as the nurse pointed to letters which he tried unsuccessfully to see with his glass eye.

Awareness of our patients' eyes is obviously very important but pediatricians also have to be sensitive to parents' eyes and parents' coded eye signals when they want the doctor to discuss something with the child without the child knowing about the parent's involvement. Sometimes this heightened awareness can lead to trouble as it did with my partner one day. While examining a five year old girl for her kindergarten check up, he noticed the mother wink at him as she told him that her daughter had been complaining of frequent stomach aches on school days. He assumed the wink to be a signal telling him to minimize the complaint which the mother probably thought represented a fear of separation when going to school rather than from a true physical ailment. He cheerfully winked back at the mother to show her that he understood her secret message as he asked the little girl to describe her "tummy aches."

The mother winked again as she explained that the complaints only happened in the morning and my partner happily winked back at her conspiratorially as he questioned the child about her appetite. The mother winked some more as she related concerns about her daughter's weight and my partner cheerily screwed up his face into an exaggerated wink to show that he had caught on as he asked the little girl about constipation. Only then did he suddenly notice to his horror that the mother was continuing to wink with what he suddenly realized was an involuntary facial tic. He quickly finished the exam and left the room as quickly as he could without having to ever find out what the mother might have thought about his winking at her throughout her daughter's exam.

The Family Livestock

MANY TIMES THE DEMANDS of a busy office, my own children, my extended family, and our household got overwhelming. There are many different stress coping mechanisms discussed at length in psychology texts but I believe mine was unique. When most overwhelmed and most depressed I'd go out and bring home another animal.

In fact when the father of one of my patients asked me to go with him to a local farm to get some baby ducks for his children I gladly went. It came as no surprise to my husband that although once there my patient's father thought twice and decided not to get any ducks, I returned home with two baby geese.

With all our animals, the chaos obviously increased but I found the distraction somehow soothing so kept adding creatures. The emotional difficulties of being a physician, wife, and mother were therefore perhaps most apparent in our family livestock count which at its peak included four horses, two geese, two dogs, a cat, a rabbit, two gerbils, 20 tropical fish, and at conservative estimate, 80 tadpoles.

There is a well known fable about a man who thought his house was too noisy with its rattling windows and creaking floor boards. He was advised to get a cow. The mooing made things worse so he was advised to also get a sheep. The baaing and mooing was still worse so he was advised to get a dog. This went on until his house was full of animals and obviously extremely noisy. He was then advised to get rid of all the animals. Returning to the same house as originally but now without the animals he was delighted to find that the place was amazingly quiet despite its still rattling windows and creaking floor boards.

That fable must have loomed large in my subconscious mind but there was a major difference between that man and me. I kept getting more animals but was then unable to part with any of them and so the level of activity and confusion at home steadily rose. At one stressful moment and as a van delivered the most recent elderly horse addition to the menagerie, my usually patient husband wondered aloud whether I might find psychotherapy cheaper and more helpful.

Nonetheless, our list of critters grew as did the realization that knowing how to treat children and their illnesses did not necessarily convey wisdom in dealing with the ailments of animals. You can imagine the embarrassment of being a physician and taking your supposedly female cat to be spayed only to have the vet tell you that she isn't a she and that one cannot spay a "he."

This ignorance of animal anatomy was again apparent when discovering after two years of ownership that the reason our pair of goslings were unable to produce eggs and more goslings was that they were both males. Similarly, our parent gerbil pair never produced young gerbils because they too were apparently both males. I did better with the tropical fish and became quite skilled at sexing the males and females of several species although it generally proved a futile observation since one of our shark like fish developed a taste for pregnant female fish and the surviving female fish developed a similar taste for their own youngsters and so our fish population remained relatively stable.

Further animal related medical humiliation awaited me when I took my cat for what I thought was a well-cat checkup only to discover that unknown to me he had a huge abscess and high fever and needed surgery. Equally upsetting was when I studied the animal care books and decided that the flaky skin on one of my horses was undoubtedly due to mange. This dreadful contagious disease could be treated only by using this foul highly toxic potion which the feed store sales clerk advised me to buy. The directions on the can were so terrifying though that after buying it I decided to have the vet make a housecall and treat the horse for me.

The vet arrived to examine the horse the next day only to shake his head in an amused fashion, collect his fee, suggest that I try to think of the horses as large furry children, and announce that the horse did not have mange at all but instead simple dandruff.

I loved all my animals but it did prove quite a challenge to care for them all while also raising our family and managing my busy medical practice. I was on call for the office every third night and every third weekend and when not on call wanted to spend as much time as possible with my children so it was sometimes hard finding enough time to ride my horse who got rather rambunctious if not ridden for too long. My father came up with the novel idea to rename my horse "Call" so that my husband could very professionally tell the answering service when they called that I couldn't be reached for an hour because I was out "on Call." I loved the idea but never did rename the horse. Instead I became friends with a veterinarian who loved to ride and agreed to ride the horse for me on days when I couldn't.

One time however she was the one on call instead of me but she wanted to ride anyway so she gave me her beeper and told me to handle the calls until she came back and that everything would be fine if I gave advice just as if the patients were small children. This worked pretty well until the time I answered a call for her about a cat that had just been hit by a car. The owners said that the cat seemed not to have any major injuries but had a bad cut and was very agitated. Clearly the cat needed to be seen so I gave the owners all the first aid advice I could think of and headed out to try to track down the vet who was riding my horse. When I finally found her she said that I had handled the situation very well but that I should have also told the owners to put the cat in a box in a dark closet until it could be seen. Apparently that that was how vets sometimes kept injured animals calm but it was certainly not anything we ever did with children.

In any case we had a lot of animals and I truly loved each one of them although it was apparently not always a mutual feeling. The rabbit got scared by some distant thunder and ran away, the geese grew older and evolved into cantankerous attack geese, and once the inside of their corral was all chewed and the grass outside their corral more lush, even the horses would take off. One eventful night that was actually the day before I delivered my second son, one of our horses escaped and went visiting a lady horse several miles away. When we received the 5:00 am call that our horse was in this other person's yard, my sleepy husband enthusiastically thanked the man who called, said we'd be right over and hung up without ever getting the address. We did manage to find the horse, however, and were able to lead it home. Since that was in the days before my husband had become comfortable handling the horses himself though and I being nine months pregnant wasn't able to ride, I had to walk the horse the several miles home on foot with my huge pregnant belly leading the way and my husband following in the car. It had still been only about 5:30 am when we had found the horse and all the way home he whinnied and neighed at every house we passed making me feel like a modern day Mrs. Paul Revere as we undoubtedly woke up every household along our route.

MOUNTAINS OF MANURE

THERE WERE OF COURSE other aspects of having animals to be dealt with and those of the horses the most challenging. The whole family learned to ride but my children were too young to help and my husband claimed to be allergic to the hay so everything horse related fell to me. Sometimes I wish I could have lived out my childhood fantasies of having loads of animals when still a child so that the concept would have been out of my system by the time I was grown. This hadn't happened, however, so at the age of 30 I found myself with a husband, two children, a house, a career, two dogs, a cat, multiple fish, a rabbit and at that time two horses.

If you've never gone to work with manure caked on your high heels and stray wisps of hay in your sweater then you also probably have no way of understanding the sinking feeling of sitting down to an elegant dinner party you're serving in your dining room only to suddenly notice through the window that your horses have escaped from their corral and are streaking across your neighbor's garden on their way to greener pastures.

The excitement of such a moment must be contagious as more than once I'd find city friends tearing out of the house with me as I'd drop my soup to run after the horses. The craziness of the scene was accentuated by hearing my friends huffing and puffing along behind me while questioning with amazement why they were running since they had no idea what on earth they would do if one of those animals got anywhere near them.

Not content to be unable to efficiently deal with two horses, I surprised my family by arriving home one day with an additional small pony who was being given away to anyone able to provide her a good home. My patient husband helped me settle her in the barn while mumbling that he was glad that no one had been giving away elephants. Having a husband and two children and two horses but just one pony it was then clear that still another pony was needed and that's how Christopher Robin came to move in with Goldie, Ben and Max.

The fun was clearly just beginning though since now my guests could be treated to the occasional thrill of four-horse breakouts and roundups. It was worth it, however, on the rare occasions that both boys and their father agreed we would all go for a ride together. These were not your everyday imagined gallops through the countryside. Each horse had its own personality to be dealt with. Ben was a huge horse who moseyed leisurely along in the rear sniffing the flowers, tasting the leaves and generally going when and where he pleased since my husband, his rider, had no inclination to argue with him.

Chris was a lively pony who went along crisply until the fields finally became too tempting at which time he buried his face in the grass, oblivious to all my older son's urgings, pleadings and insistences that he move.

Goldie our small Shetland pony behaved well with my youngest son aboard until she would decide that her small legs had gone far enough. At that point, whether in a field, in the middle of the road, or in a puddle, she would plant her feet and refuse to budge unless it was in the direction of home. She was too well trained to bolt for the barn but would instead slowly turn around and slowly, but with determination, head for home leaving the other horses to continue without her if they were foolish enough to want to get more exhausted.

No ride was therefore ever totally uneventful but by far the most dramatic conclusion was the ride on which Ben tried crossing a small shallow stream behind our house only to suddenly sink in mud halfway up his back. With his legs stuck deep in the mud he couldn't move at all and so being an old fatalistic horse, he promptly closed his eyes and put his head down ready to drown if that was what was required of him. I quickly got a log to put under his head and hold it out of the water until I could get help but beyond that I was pretty terrified because I had no idea how anyone would ever be able to get him out since he was a huge horse and completely unable to move his legs because of the thick mud. At that point in time I was letting a local teenager use my horse as her 4-H project and she happened to stop by while this was going on. Her level of participation was that after seeing the horse in the mud, she collapsed onto a nearby log and sat there crying for the next several hours.

We had also just hired a new housecleaner at an exorbitant hourly rate and hearing the commotion in the woods she had run out of the house to see what was happening and promptly spent the next few hours standing near the horse praying. Meanwhile I rang the local fire department to see if they could help. When they arrived it was truly quite a scene but maybe all the praying and crying did somehow help because 2 hours later after 10 firemen had been pulling this way and that with various ropes and pulleys, we finally did get Ben out of the mud. The humans were pretty shaken by the whole ordeal but surprisingly Ben was totally fine although he never voluntarily walked through any puddles ever again.

Another equally memorable though much less dramatic ride was one which resulted in my returning home dripping wet since my horse Max had decided that merely drinking from a trailside lake would only quench his thirst whereas rolling in it despite my still being in the saddle on his back would cool him off completely.

Having the horses also resulted in an unforeseen medical challenge because after one bizarre riding accident described in a later chapter in which I broke my ankle I was placed in a long groin to foot rigid cast. Not only did the inflexibility of the cast make me occasionally get stuck in the tiny office bathroom unable to open the door but it also made examining newborns at the hospital a real challenge because the newborn baby carts were all on wheels. I couldn't use my crutches while examining patients because I needed my hands free but I was unable to put any weight on my casted leg. This posed a real dilemma because I was also unable to balance too long on just one foot but I solved it by leaning on the carts while examining the babies. Sometimes this worked out fine but other times the cart would start rolling across the room with me attached making simply staying upright as much of a challenge as examining the baby.

In any case despite my injury and the added challenge it provided I loved having the horses and once my ankle had healed the family did have a number of fun rides together. One day however the ordinarily tranquil rides through the picturesque fall foliage became transformed by the vote of our suburban townsfolk to allow hunting in the conservation areas which were places where we often liked to ride. Now instead of the soft whisper of breezes through the leaves and the quiet clip clop of the horses' feet, passerbys would hear bells jangling on the horses' bridles to warn hunters of our approach as well as my riding partner's repetitive shouts of , "Don't shoot, don't shoot, we're not ducks."

I always remained fascinated with the horses, however, and also intrigued by their individual personalities which were similar in many ways to people I knew. Ben was built like a Sherman tank and ate everything in sight. He was a quiet, gentle animal but at feeding time he had to be fed first or he instantly underwent a complete metamorphosis into a savage beast, biting and kicking any animal within range. If he finished his meal and heard the other horses still eating he would become furious enough to totally kick down the entire outside wall of the barn. This unfortunately happened often and the feat delighted my carpenter whom I suspect was getting rich by his frequent visits to reattach the barn wall.

Max, on the other hand, was docile and generous. He was forever skin and bones since he was unwilling to argue with anyone who wanted any of his food. Although twice the size of the ponies he would readily step aside to let them eat his dinner if they decided it smelled better than theirs. The stall doors were always open to the field so that the horses could go in and out at will. They each knew which stall was theirs and rarely entered the wrong one but if ever one of the other horses did decide to take over Max's stall, he'd gracefully back out and stand in the rain rather than make a fuss.

The littlest pony, Goldie, acted like a spoiled baby. She delighted in trying to get the others in trouble. If she saw me coming she would walk over to one of the other horses and whinny frantically as if he had just hurt her and then run over to me as if to have me save her. All in all though the horses got along well and must have really liked being here as much as I liked having them since they absolutely refused to ever get on any trailer, van or truck and therefore could never be sold.

Thus, the future entailed our continued enjoyment of riding and watching our four horses as the mountains of manure grew and grew almost obscuring our view.

PUFF

IN ADDITION TO THE horses, geese, gerbils, cat, and fish, we of course also had to have a dog and in later years even had two of them at the same time. Our first dogs weren't too large and when we moved to the suburbs would unfortunately be harassed by our neighbor's much larger German Shepherd. This made our sons want an even bigger dog and we went around looking at St Bernards, Great Danes, Newfoundlands and other large breed puppies totally ignoring the fact that when full grown none of them would fit into our small Ford Pinto wagon.

None seemed quite right for us though until we spotted an Old English Sheepdog. Have you ever admired those gorgeous, fluffy, white and grey Old English Sheepdogs as they majestically parade down the avenue at their owner's side? Well, I had always dreamed of owning one ever since my Lassie phase ended at about 18. However, it wasn't until I was married with two small children, a career, and a house in the country that I found myself finally able to fulfill this dream.

My family selected an adorable small white and black ball of fluff which leapt all over us like a motorized stuffed animal. Once home, we quickly discovered that "Puff", as we named him, could also leap over gates, suitcases, and sofas whenever he felt the urge to pee on the rug. He was a lovable sweet dog though and did eventually become somewhat housebroken as he grew and grew and grew into what eventually was the largest and strongest sheep dog I had ever seen.

Grooming a dog that size and that lively was really a chore. Puff had to be wrestled to the ground and brushed while being sat on. He found this great fun as he rolled around trying to chew the brush and lick the groomer. We finally gave up and just had him shaved in the spring. He saw better with the hair off his face anyway and stopped falling down the stairs plus we had the additional benefit of three dogs for the price of one as he transformed into a "Greyhound" each spring, partially regrew his coat and became an "Airedale" each fall and finally regained his full coat and returned to being a sheepdog each winter. Although not too well behaved he was still a very sweet huge huggable dog and became a neighborhood favorite. I couldn't find any dog houses his size so the children helped me build him a huge one but in Puff's own unique style he refused to ever go into the dog house and instead became a familiar sight sitting on its roof like Snoopy while calmly surveying the passerbys.

My long held dream was complete each day as Puff and I walked my sons to the corner to catch the school bus. Puff, however, took this task literally and if there hadn't been a large fire hydrant handy for me to grab as an anchor we'd still be tearing through town trying to catch the school bus. In fact, the only thing Puff liked to try to catch was the bus. He loved watching me throw a ball and wagged his rump furiously with delight as I retrieved the ball but no amount of coaxing could get him to try the game himself. We bought hollow balls which we filled with hamburger meat and hard balls which we buttered, and rubber bones, squeaky mice and old socks. However, the only thing Puff was ever interested in chasing was the school bus.

We eventually decided that he was trying to tell us he needed help so we took him to obedience school. There were cute little poodles, seriously attentive shepherds and quick learning terriers; and then there was Puff. When the instructor said "Get down on your knees next to your dog" to show him how to sit and I attempted that maneuver Puff saw it as a cue to show his affection and all one hundred pounds of him leapt on top of me, licking and rolling around until we were both lathered with mud and saliva. When the instructor said to call "come" and pull your dog toward you, my dog sat down wagging his rump in delight as I unsuccessfully tried to reel him in and had to finally resort to going over myself to where he sat. The classes were successful in some bizarre way though since he did wind up learning some new commands but with his own unique twist in that he finished the classes having learned that "sit" meant play and "come" meant sit.

We next tried sending him to a week at a doggy boarding school. This was as much a mistake as it was humiliating. Puff flunked out of the school but only after learning that when we called "come", instead of stopping where he was and sitting down to wait for us to go get him as he had done before, he now heard the word "come", gave us a gleeful look and bounded away in the opposite direction. This obviously added to the fun at home especially when the school bus came.

Additionally, those elegant pictures of sheep dogs never show them candidly at home on an average day and certainly never after they've been near a swamp. Unfortunately, our house bordered a swamp with all its neat smells and wildlife to entice a dog to explore. The fact is that when a sheep dog gets into a swamp he turns into the hugest smelliest mud ball imaginable. It was when Puff was outside happily in such a state one day that I called him. Just at that moment the school bus also arrived on our street. With delighted leaps Puff ran away from me, boarded the bus, and seated himself, to everyone's astonishment, in the last row. As I claimed this foul-smelling delinquent I couldn't bring myself to admit that he was mine and could only manage to mumble that I know his owner and would take him home.

Despite the lure of the swamp. Puff generally stayed near us wherever we were but sometimes he'd get distracted and wander off and on those occasions the swamp wasn't the only mischievous place he'd visit. We put up a fence all around our yard but Puff would either dig under or jump over so we tried tying him. We discovered, however, that some animals are just not meant to be restrained as Puff chewed through ropes, snapped off dog chains and finally uprooted the heavy link chain we were trying and gleefully dragged the entire length of it up to the nearby high school. There he tried to be one of the students as he watched football practice on sunny days and gymnastics in the gym on rainy days, munched on students' lunches during recess and even swiped cookies from the principal's office when he wanted dessert. The teachers who called us to come get him always seemed more amused than upset but life with Puff was definitely wild as the multiple daytime calls from the school were matched by the frequent night time chaos at home as my son would often wake up crying with the bad dream of being attached by a bear only to discover when fully awake that it was just Puff who had leapt onto his bed to give him a lick and stand guard. .

Mealtimes with a dog that size were unusual too. When Puff stood under the table he was so large that when he obeyed the command to go out of the room and lie down, the table moved with him. When he sat next to the table his chin rested on it. My husband would tell him to stop begging and to sit only to realize with dismay that the poor dog was already sitting. Even when not eating the household was in a constant state of alert as we learned to be ready to flatten ourselves against the closest wall at a moment's notice if Puff ever caught sight of our cat and wanting to play charged headlong after him ignoring all people and objects in his path.

Having a dog that size was clearly a challenge but it did also have some added benefits because although Puff was a totally sweet incredibly affectionate dog without a mean bone in his body, his very size could be intimidating to strangers. With Puff in our family, our neighbor's German Shepherd who had terrorized our last much smaller dog never even entered our yard anymore and when workmen came into the house they would work quickly while giving me and the dog a fearful wide berth not knowing that the only risk they would have faced if they had gotten too close to Puff would have been getting licked to death.

Later dogs provided challenges too. Most of our dogs had been adopted from shelters: Luvie, Sparky, Oreo, Mr Magoo, Tundra, Pudge, and Nicky. They were all terrific dogs but like all dogs several did develop medical problems. At one time we had two older dogs both of which had developed diabetes and needed individualized varying insulin doses depending on the degree of sugar in their urine. It was hard catching a urine sample from them especially since they would each immediately stop peeing and glare at me whenever I tried to sneak a cup under them while they were trying to pee. It made my mornings especially hard when each day before leaving for the office I had to get samples from each of them, test the samples, calculate their dose of insulin and give them their shot. Added to that was the fact that one dog was deaf and the other blind. I once applied for long term care insurance and a nurse from the insurance company called me to run through some routine questions before approving my application. She asked whether I ever had trouble getting out of the house in the morning, whether I ever had trouble with medication, and whether I felt I needed a nurse to help me and to each question I said that I definitely felt I did need help. She sounded pretty shocked that with so much difficulty I had thought I could qualify for the insurance but before she could hang up and reject my application, I explained that my answers were all because of the dogs and that I was actually perfectly healthy but could definitely use a nurse to help with the dogs.

This became an even greater need with the last dog we had. He was a wonderful lovable dog who had been rescued as a puppy from a garbage dump in Puerto Rico and taken to a shelter in the US where we had adopted him and named him Nicky because we had gotten to the shelter in the "nick of time."

Nicky went everyplace with us and we had many years of wonderful times together but he did have one difficult idiosyncrasy in addition to a lifelong fear of garbage trucks. He was extremely protective of me and would charge at my husband if he ever tried to give me a hug. If Nicky ever even heard the words, "give me a hug" he'd race over to attack my husband. This sometimes posed a challenge but actually became the easiest way to call him in from outside. I'd stand at the door and yell "give me a hug, oh please come give me a hug" at the top of my lungs and Nicky would stop whatever he was doing and race back to the house. I suspect hearing me loudly calling this out several times a day must have been a bit startling for our neighbors but it definitely got results from Nicky.

Nicky was otherwise a truly wonderful dog but in his old age he developed congestive heart failure and I had to get up multiple times a night to give him medication and when he got weaker to carry him outside to pee. It was exhausting and a nurse definitely would have helped. He remained a sweet happy dog despite his illness however and his eventual death was devastating. My husband told me that I wouldn't be able to survive another such loss and so we shouldn't get any more dogs. I was actively doing animal rights work at the time and used to take Nicky with me when I gave talks so felt I definitely needed some kind of animal. The rest of my family was allergic to cats so I decided to get a rabbit. My husband thought that that was a great idea because he didn't think I'd get attached to a rabbit and so we wouldn't have to travel with it. Needless to say he was very wrong and our bunny is known at motels all up and down the coast since she's always with us on trips to Vermont and Florida.

Looking on the Bright Side

DESPITE ALL THE ANIMALS, we did also like to take trips and although hard, we did somehow always manage to find housesitters willing to cope with our menagerie so that we could travel. Some parents take trips without their children but our family always traveled together to make up for our times apart due to our demanding work schedules. We've had many wonderful travels filled with fun, swimming, tennis, friendship and laughs but many trips held unexpected excitement.

The tone of family trips was set early on in Cape May, New Jersey at a charming old hotel on the ocean when our oldest son was still a toddler. The ocean and beach were wonderful and the hotel lovely but it was hardly a restful vacation because our son absolutely would not go to sleep. I couldn't blame him though since things started off on the wrong foot the very first night we were there when he absolutely refused to get into the crib supplied by the hotel.

We tried all sorts of inducements and eventually after much persuading finally convinced him to climb into the strange looking crib so we could all go to sleep. It wasn't long though before a crash and his screams woke us up as the crib suddenly collapsed showing him that parents do not know everything and that he had been completely right to refuse to sleep in that crazy looking thing in the first place.

Subsequent trips included eternity's of time while I sat on the toilet and my husband on the edge of the bathtub, both holding our breaths and listening for our children to settle down to sleep in the strange beds in the totally dark bedroom. Any movement on our part, whispered conversation or flashlight to read would cause little heads to pop up asking if it was morning yet. I can probably still trace out all the floor tile patterns memorized during my hours of quietly waiting in bathrooms all up and down the east coast of America.

Hotels were not the only challenge, however. One memorable trip to Florida by train was booked by a sleepy travel agent who must have not heard me say that we needed a sleeper car for three. Being nine months pregnant at the time with our second child, it was difficult to squeeze through the narrow doorway into our closet-sized train compartment but once inside it was even more shocking to realize that the tiny room only had two seats and a toilet. Since husbands like comfort and no one argues with a four year old if they can avoid it, I found myself sitting on a toilet most of the two day trip to Florida. At night the two chairs became a bed for one and an additional bed pulled out of the wall above. If your arithmetic is good you will realize that once again I was probably destined to sleep on the toilet.

During the first night I did try sleeping in my son's bed while holding on to the nearby opposite wall so I wouldn't fall out but needless to say with a nine-month pregnant tummy near him, my son found the bed too cramped and after an hour said that he was no longer afraid and could now sleep alone. Back I went to the toilet. The fact that the train's heating system malfunctioned and remained on full force all the way to Miami naturally added to our enjoyment of the trip.

Car travels were also not without troubles. These trips held varied kinds of difficulties. The mildest but obviously still chaotic trip was our five hour drive from Washington to New York one Sunday during which our poor infant son had diarrhea and I had to change 12 – I kept count to stay sane – dirty diapers all on my lap since we couldn't find any open rest rooms.

Another eventful drive was our tired Pinto wagon's last family trip. We got excellent highway gas mileage because I recall that we were towed further than we drove and visited scenic service stations in each state we passed. The trip had initially started out uneventfully until I got hungry and announced a craving for Kentucky Fried Chicken. As if it had ears the car promptly coughed to a stall. When we finally reached the AAA and got a tow to the closest garage we found ourselves in a desolate area with no store or restaurant of any sort for miles except for a Kentucky Fried Chicken Restaurant directly across the street. There we spent a pleasant breakfast, somewhat impatient lunch, and very agitated dinner while the mechanic waited for the delivery of the part he claimed our car needed. Our car limped along for the rest of the drive in a relatively uneventful manner but I had definitely learned the lesson to be careful what you wish for.

Of course now that trip would have been even more stressful than it was back then since as I said earlier, these days I'm vegetarian and wouldn't have been able to eat the chicken at all.

In any case we had many other very exciting drives including the one to Florida right through the heart of the 1983 blizzard where we were forced to turn and drive north on the south bound side of the highway to get past the large number of snow bound cars in front of us.

In case you've been wondering, we did occasionally try traveling by air but it never quite worked out either since basically I'm one of those people who feel that if God had meant me to fly he'd have given me wings. To stay calm on a plane I'd pretend it was a train. This worked great until I had children. My son would pull up the shades, look out the plane window and point out clouds that I'd try to insist were not clouds but farm houses as I tried to pull the shade back down.

As we circled for a landing he'd look down and ask how the plane would land and whether it would just "crash right down there." We did keep trying to fly though until the time we had terrible turbulence and circled the airport for so long that our crated dog's tranquilizer wore off and she came within two fat splinters of chewing her way totally free in the baggage compartment.

Trips were unusual even once we arrived at our destination. One skiing vacation drive to a mountain at the Canadian border revealed warmer weather and less snow the further north we went. We had pictured a quaint ski lodge with a Christmas tree in the lounge and relaxing with friends around the fireplace after a full day of fun in the snow.

Instead we arrived at a lodge which was apparently taken completely by surprise at our arrival since with no snow all their other guests had wisely canceled. The management hastily set up the undecorated Christmas tree and lit the fire to make the empty inn seem at least a bit more festive and we wound up sitting in the conversational fire pit making small talk with the two dogs and three cats who were the only living beings sharing the lodge and who had promptly stretched out taking over the most comfortable spots.

The owner of the inn tried to make things nice for us but I'm not sure when the inn had actually last had any guests at all because our room was dusty and stale with rickety furnishings. The lamps were all without light bulbs too except for one lamp in the far left hand corner. My husband and I were pretty upset but being an optimistic good natured child, our older son told us to stop complaining and to try to look on the bright side. When we asked what was the bright side, our younger son said that it was probably the far left hand corner of the room which had the lamp.

A discussion of our trips is not complete without mentioning our many wonderful trips with our close friends from Cincinnati. Our two children were good friends with their three and we shared many warm close times together. The trips with them to Florida were especially "close" since their car usually broke down as soon as it arrived in Florida and we would have to cram the four of us and five of them into our small Pinto wagon. People watched us pile out of the car as if we were clowns from the circus.

With five small children in our combined families we found it necessary to make dinner reservations under different names each night to be sure they'd allow us to come back. I still feel badly about the young waitress who tried to take our order one night until after the second child changed her mind for the third time and the third child changed his mind for the second time and the milk had spilled for a further time. The waitress then excused herself, got her sweater, quit her job and left the restaurant.

These trips with our friends were, however, made much more meaningful by the many interests and patient explanations of the family's father who was a scientist. Many an evening was enhanced, although lengthened, as we rushed to get somewhere with the hour late and the children hot and cranky only to have our friend suddenly tell us to quickly pull off the road and immediately all get out of the car. The supposed crisis usually turned out to be his simply wanting to show us some unusual roadside plant or night time galaxy.

The sights were always exciting and well worth seeing but piling five cranky sunburnt children back into our small car was always a challenge. Our friend's desire to share his enthusiasm for nature was only once regretted. That was the time in Kentucky when he caught a huge box turtle while the rest of us were off horseback riding. He thought it fascinating and wanted to show it to us and so kept it in his car waiting until we returned from or ride. Afterwards, as he hosed down the now filthy smelly mats from what had been his spanking clean brand new car, we learned the unusual nature lesson of how very many times a frightened turtle can move its bowels in the back of a station wagon over the course of two hours.

PATIENTS AND PATIENCE

OUR FAMILY TRIPS WERE wonderful highlights but back home the challenges of office pediatrics continued. Many of these were unusual and completely unanticipated. People react differently at times of stress and many of the interactions with patients or with parents were far from anything taught in textbooks. As the waiting room got increasingly packed parents would get understandably increasingly annoyed. A nurse's simple query of, "What's the matter with your baby?" would often get the hostile response of, "If I knew I wouldn't be here" instead of a helpful clue that he had a fever or a cough or a red toe.

Our office established a custom of having the nurse jot down a child's main complaint on a pad outside the examining room door to save physician time and help the doctor know which child was more acutely ill and so would need to be seen first.

One memorable day early in my career I entered an examining room which contained a new mother and her six week old baby. The note on the door by error still listed the previous day's complaint of a different child who had had a high fever and sore throat. The note had nothing to do with the smiling cooing baby on the examining table but I was unaware of the error. As I approached this adorable thriving infant I casually mentioned to the mother that I gathered that the baby had had a high fever the previous night. New mothers often revere the lofty insights and presumed infallible wisdom of their pediatricians. Therefore, when I commented on the baby's fever of the night before, the mother, who should have known that her baby was entirely well, instantly assumed that my medical skills had detected a serious problem which she had stupidly missed. She looked horrorstruck and concerned as she asked, "he did?"

I was puzzled at her reaction but her obvious concern made me continue by asking her again about the baby's fever. At this she worriedly asked me how high it had been? I decided to change tactics and try to find out what had made her decide that a baby that small had had a sore throat. Horrified to have been such an unobservant mother and to have missed her child's first illness, she stammered, "Well, I really wasn't sure," followed by her asking me whether his throat would be all right.

At this point I finally realized that something very odd was going on and so excused myself to speak to the nurse. She explained to me the error in the note on the door. When I returned to the examining room to explain the misunderstanding to the mother I found that no degree of reassurance could convince her that her baby was in fact well and had not had a high fever and sore throat the previous night. She continued to hover worriedly over her smiling bouncing baby and to apologize for not noticing promptly his fever and sore throat.

At one point in time our waiting room was shared with a local gynecologist and obstetrician. I always tried hard not to keep patients waiting although some days it was unavoidable because of the sheer number needing to be seen that day. Most days therefore the waiting room was orderly and sharing it with the gynecologist obstetrician worked well until one extremely busy day when the impatiently waiting children were getting increasingly wild and noisy. Suddenly I noticed an agitated young woman who had been sitting for over an hour in the waiting room waiting for her scheduled gynecology appointment at which she had apparently planned to have her IUD removed so she could start a family. As the children around her threw crayons and roared imaginary fire trucks and the hungry babies began crying all at the same time, I saw her suddenly rise, go over to the desk and cancel her appointment saying that she had decided to reconsider parenthood. Needless to say, the gynecologist shortly thereafter relocated his office.

Our staff, however, loved working with the children and we all found their innocent remarks refreshing. While examining one small baby I noticed his small sister playing quietly in the corner with her baby doll. Having learned how to care for an infant in the twentieth century she was engrossed in nursing her doll. I overheard her solemnly explain as she switched the doll from one side of her chest to the other, "There, that one was for milk and this one is for juice."

I clearly also remember one little girl in the waiting room who kept getting into trouble trying to feed her new infant brother part of her sandwich. Her exasperated mother and grandmother explained for the umpteenth time that the baby couldn't share her food because he had no teeth yet. The little girl pondered briefly and then, apparently recalling the times she had seen grandma remove and wash her dentures, she brightly blurted out through the entire quiet waiting room, "Why don't we lend the baby grandma's teeth so he can share my cookie."

One of my favorite reactions to the waiting room scene though was provided by my father. He had gone to consult a busy surgical specialist and had been kept waiting in the waiting room for over two hours before being seen by the doctor. When finally in the examining room the doctor proceeded to start taking the standard medical history and asked him, "How old are you?" To which my father pleasantly replied, "Do you mean now or when I first came in?"

What Did You Say?

OTHER PECULIARITIES OF PEDIATRIC practice were caused by problems in communication. After years of training it's sometimes hard to remember how strange medical terms and procedures must appear to non-physicians and particularly to children. It's hard to forget the horrified look on the face of the ill child having a throat culture as the nurse explained that we needed to take the culture swab in order to get some of the bugs from his throat. The boy became pale and nauseated as he yelled, "Yech! There are insects crawling in my mouth."

On the medical side, no matter how hectic the day, it's important for nurses and physicians to slow down and always fully listen to patients and not jump to conclusions based on a faulty understanding of what was said.

One memorable evening early in my training I was on duty in the emergency room when a young teenager gave birth to a baby alone at home and called the hospital to ask what she should do. She sounded terribly alarmed on the phone saying that she had just given birth and that the baby was lying there on the sofa, not moving, not crying, not anything. The emergency room nurse assumed from this that the baby had been born dead and so she calmly advised the girl that everything would be taken care of and to put the baby in a paper bag and to come with it by taxi to the hospital. A few minutes later I walked by the emergency room entrance as a young girl entered carrying a brown paper bag under her arm from which emitted very lusty cries and kicks. Shortly after hanging up the phone, the unquestioning new mother had realized her baby was alive but had assumed that the emergency room staff knew best how to transport a newborn infant and so had put the baby, as suggested, in a paper bag to carry it to the hospital.

When dealing with large numbers of people it's inevitable that simple questions will sometimes have different interpretations and so result in strange answers. I recall a friend of mine delivering her first child in the days before husbands were allowed in the delivery room and before parents were told the sex of their baby from ultrasounds. After my friend gave birth she was wheeled on a stretcher out of the delivery room past her nervously pacing husband. He rushed over to his wife and anxiously asked, "What did we have?" She smiled serenely at him before falling asleep as she answered, "It was a baby."

Children's literal interpretations of questions can often be very refreshing too. When examining small children I often liked to involve them in conversation to distract them and to also hear the quality of their speech. Frequently I'd ask a child what was his favorite thing to eat. To the embarrassment of parents, I've received answers ranging from "spinach and steak" to "candy and sugar" with the usual three year old winner being, "Pisghetti" and one true child of the 90's answering "Takeout."

One day I asked a toddler what he liked most to eat and I received the prompt answer, "Food." He then solemnly added that he ate it for breakfast, lunch, and dinner. When I persisted by asking which was his favorite food, he thought quietly a while and then responded, "Lunch."

Parents are often unfamiliar with medical terms which I totally understand since I'm not familiar with the terms used in other professions but sometimes this lack of knowledge can be quite funny. One time I had a Greek family come to the office with their child and while there the father asked me if I could weigh in on a problem his nephew was having back in Greece that was mystifying all the doctors there. He said that he felt American doctors were probably smarter so had told his brother that he'd ask me. He then went on to describe his nephew having strange looking red blotches all over his body. I told him that his nephew had a rash of some sort and that without seeing it myself there was no way I could diagnose it. At hearing that, he looked delighted and said. "A "rash"!! You said what he had was a "rash"! I just knew you'd know."

Sometimes I'd be the one misunderstanding the patient. I'll never forget the time I met a young boy with severe asthma at the office in the middle of the night. The boy was wheezing pretty badly and in those days the standard treatment was a shot of epinephrine. Usually the nurses gave the shots in our office but I had certainly done it in medical school and although that had been a number of years ago I was sure I could still do it.

I calculated the dose carefully, drew up the solution, and gave the boy the prescribed amount. The epinephrine shots usually took several minutes to work but were almost always very effective although often had side effects ranging from unpleasant nausea to worrisome racing hearts. I stood watching the boy and chatting with the father while waiting for the medicine to take effect when the boy who had been listless and breathing hard suddenly announced, "I feel strange." I tried to stay calm as I checked and rechecked the bottle of epinephrine to be sure I had given the correct dose while the boy sat there repeating over and over that he was feeling really really strange. Just when I was thinking I should call for an ambulance, the boy suddenly leaped off the examining room table and announced "I feel like dancing!" Clearly the medicine had opened up his airway and the strange feeling he had had was that he was now suddenly feeling totally fine. He and his father were delighted. His wheezing had completely stopped and his heart rate was fine but it took me quite a while more to get my own heart rate under control.

Meanwhile parents can be misunderstood as well as patients. In medicine the slang term for a seizure or a convulsion would be a "fit." Therefore, when a mother called one day frantic about her child having a prolonged fit which wouldn't stop, my partner assumed the child was having a seizure. Due to the prolonged nature of the fit and the mother's increasing concern and panic on the phone he was just about to arrange for immediate transportation to the hospital when the mother added that the child's fit had started when she wouldn't give him a cookie and he had been kicking his feet and screaming at her ever since.

SUPERMOM

MANY WORKING WOMEN CAN attest to the difficulty of being a super mom, a woman who deftly juggles home, children, and career from morning through night without sleep for weeks on end. Add to the usual pressures on such a woman the weight of high expectations from those who look on her as an expert on all matters related to children and you have the complete picture of a mother-pediatrician. This obviously created a lot of emotional stress when my own children were ill and I wanted to be home with them but had a waiting room full of other sick children.

It was also a problem in relationships with friends. There weren't many children on the block where we lived so I had joined a playgroup so that my pre-school child could be with other children. These groups were also wonderful for the mothers who could share their concerns and frustrations with other people facing the same issues. In my case, I couldn't. As a pediatrician I was supposed to have all the answers and so never felt comfortable sharing any child raising concerns of my own. Although being very social and having many friends, this made the friendships somewhat one sided and left me feeling somewhat lonely.

My being a pediatrician also caused problems with the school nurse at my son's school. One extremely busy day while worrying about a critically ill newborn at the hospital and dealing with a packed waiting room full of sick children I received a call from the school nurse saying that my younger son was in her office with a tummy ache. From her description of the symptoms I decided it wasn't anything serious but quickly calculated that by working double-time, skipping lunch, and seeing the current office patients promptly without distractions I could pick him up at school in a little over an hour, take care of him, and return to the office only a half hour behind schedule. As I relayed this to the school nurse and hung up the phone I overheard her telling my son that it must be hard having a mommy who's a doctor because she clearly never believes you're really sick. Hearing that made my blood boil but when I raced to the school later that day to pick up my son I was vindicated and of course delighted to learn that my son hadn't had anything serious and had gotten better as predicted so had returned to class.

Other days I got the opposite response from the school. When I went to the school to pick up my truly ill child I would invariably get grinned at with the comment that the staff thought doctors' children weren't supposed to get sick.

On the other side of the coin though was the fact that my son's teacher at the time believed totally in my medical skills and wouldn't listen to anybody else including her own internist. She once called me in the middle of the school day hysterically crying. She was initially unable to even stop crying long enough to tell me the problem and for what seemed like an eternity all I could think was that something terrible must have happened to my child. After several panicked moments during which I tried to calm her down enough so that she could talk, she eventually told me that my son was fine but that she was calling for advice for herself because she had just been stung by some bees at recess and was in terrible pain.

On a different note, there were other very different non medical problems in being a working mom. These stemmed from the sudden late night or early morning remembrances of my usually otherwise fairly organized children. One example was the frequent 9:00 pm urgent request for magazine clippings or poster boards for a project due the following day and conveniently forgotten until bedtime. Another time my son suddenly remembered when he woke up that he was supposed to be in a classroom skit that day. During a frenzied breakfast ten minutes before the bus was due to arrive and while I was searching for his sneakers under the sofa, he announced that I had to make him into a bear. Having become used to these magical requests I was able to draw a bear's head on a paper bag with my right hand while feeding the dog with my left, grabbing my stethoscope off the floor with my toe and getting my son to school as a bear and myself to work without growling like one.

When the kids were older one great worry of mine was that being given a second chance at grammar school through my children might result in my losing my own high school diploma as I tried diligently to help my sons with math and my seventh grade niece with social studies. Those who talk about the difficulty of medical school probably never dealt with a teacher like the one who gave my niece a C for the beautiful and completely accurate map we had slaved over together for hours and which showed all the required early explorer routes of travel but on which we had forgotten to draw the usually present imaginary sea serpent of early maps.

As I struggled with defining monarchies and democracies interspersed with phone calls about mononucleosis and croup, and as I helped draw cones and pyramids with one hand while calculating antibiotic dosages with the other, I began to doubt the sanity of being a mother and a professional and pondered how my patients would react if I flunked the seventh grade.

Meanwhile. although working, I tried to be a good mother by volunteering for all class trips which fell on my days off. These were thoroughly enjoyable though far from restful. One favorite school trip was the fall trip to the local apple orchard. One of these was one I will never forget. It was a gorgeous, crisp day as a bus load of three kindergarten classes and six mothers all set off with the teachers to pick apples. Everything was going smoothly until one unfortunate little boy stepped on a fallen beehive.

The ensuing bedlam was unbelievable as bees swarmed out of the hive landing on children. Seventy children ran shrieking in all directions to escape the furious bees stripping off their clothes while they ran. Fortunately no one was allergic but instead of being an idyllic exploration of nature, the rest of the trip was spent looking through the woods for cowering youngsters who had run off to hide, retrieving the many fallen items of clothing the children had ripped off while running, and dabbing mud on the multiple stings of several children.

To cement my fond recollection of bees was the repeat performance at my office one year later. Two little toddlers were playing outside the office with grandma while I examined their new baby brother inside with their mom. Suddenly the children burst into the packed waiting room screaming and stripping off their clothes, and horrifying the other waiting children, parents, and nurses as bees flew out of their clothes and all over the office. As the shrieking of the stung toddlers and screaming of all the terrified waiting room children reached a crescendo I overheard my partner calmly ask, "Why can't Dr. Peppercorn control her patients?"

Of course much later I had a further bee encounter when my toddler age granddaughter was stung by a bee in her backyard and started crying. I didn't want her frightened by the bee and scared to be outside so I tried soothing her by telling that the bee hadn't meant to hurt her and that it was just the bee's way of saying "hello." A few minutes later when my husband saw her still sniffling he told her not to worry because he was going to find that bee and kill it for having hurt her. Being the incredibly sweet sensitive girl then as she still is now, she quickly told him to please not hurt the bee because it had all been her fault for not having said hello first.

Meanwhile the challenges went on but I quickly learned that efficiency was key when trying to deal with the multiple demands of being both a physician and a mother. To that end I was especially delighted one winter to have managed to buy my sons' teachers their Christmas presents of chocolates and stationery very early long before needed. The gifts were wrapped and addressed and put aside all ready and waiting for the Christmas holiday.

The night before the start of school vacation I put the gifts on the counter so as not to forget them in the morning and dashed out to pick my son up at basketball. I returned later well after the stores had all closed only to discover our delighted dog with a chocolate-stained face sitting in the living room surrounded by wrapping paper. She had not only happily devoured all the teachers' chocolates but had also chewed open the stationery boxes for a taste of those as well. When he could be heard over my wailing, my younger son helpfully suggested that maybe the teachers wouldn't notice the teeth marks in the stationery and might just think it came that way.

Meanwhile competition among parents is mild compared with the competition among children. My son always gave unsolicited reports that so and so's mother was prettier, uglier, fatter, thinner, more stylish, less stylish, older, younger, a better cook or a worse cook than me. None of it phased me except the comparison category of "yellers." Some families were very soft spoken with rather flat emotions whether for good or bad but my emotions always ran high with more hugs, praise, and I love you's but also more frustrated annoyance and yelling.

When feeling overworked and frustrated I regularly let off steam like a tea kettle so my children were often subjected to my sporadic yelling. In fact, knowing my explosive tendencies but having a sense of humor about it I had put a sign on our kitchen wall saying, "Beware, occupant may lose control without warning." However, I was sorry to have my son tell me one day that the only mother he knew who yelled more than I did was planning to move to Ohio and that I had therefore won the Massachusetts State title. Fortunately, as my sons grew older and visited more friends' homes and so met more parents and as I grew older and less harried, my boys found many more better yellers than me and so I was happily finally able to retire my title.

THE RECEIVING END

IT ISN'T ONLY DIFFICULT being a mother-pediatrician but it is also difficult being a pediatrician-mother. When I was on the receiving end of medical care some professionals neglected to acknowledge my medical knowledge while others neglected to acknowledge my inability to be objective about my own children and gave me too much responsibility for decisions about their health. It began when I was in labor and anxiously noticing ominous fetal monitor patterns which I knew meant that my baby was in potential danger and had to be delivered quickly. Having worked right up until just prior to delivery I knew that my knowledge was current and the need for concern was real. My obstetrician, however, tried to convince me not to worry by telling me that the monitor tracings no longer meant what they used to mean. It was hardly consoling to meditate on the remote possibility that the art of interpreting fetal monitors might have been totally changed in the previous day and a half.

When my children were sick I worried like any other parent and perhaps even more so since all the possible remote complications of their illnesses and medications were well known to me. It was certainly extremely difficult to be objective about one's own child when he was the one having severe croup or high fevers and hallucinations. My partners would often have their wives bring their children to the office for objective medical advice. However, my husband worked in Boston so usually couldn't come home to do the same for me. It was quite a strange feeling to be a pediatrician one minute and then reenter the waiting room a few minutes later with my own child who was coming to be seen by my partner. On one particularly stressful day my son who was at that time still an infant, was severely ill with diarrhea and dehydration. This evolved on a weekend when I was the only doctor on call for my practice. Knowing my child probably needed hospitalization but knowing he'd be terribly stressed and miserable in the hospital, I just could not bring myself to make the decision to admit him so brought him to a pediatrician in another town.

The doctor was a kindly gentleman and probably a very good doctor but deferred to me by hesitantly asking, "Will your child mind being examined by me?" I looked at my severely ill baby and tried to remain calm as I informed the doctor that my son was really sick and I had traveled a long distance to see him so really didn't care whether or not my son minded being examined and to please just do it.

The pediatrician then checked my son and told me, as I knew deep down, that he should probably be hospitalized but that he would leave the decision up to me. The only thing worse than having the decision I had driven miles to avoid having to make myself being thrust back into my lap, was my being told later after having finally admitted my son to the hospital with his continued watery diarrhea that the pediatric floor had just run out of diapers.

Other physicians were also usually very candid with me about my children's health though sometimes physicians spoke too frankly not realizing that I had entered their office with my stethoscope and medical mind parked outside and only my marshmallow mommy heart with me. For example I once tried to obtain a second opinion about my son's possible need for radical head surgery following an accidental injury to his orbital area. Forgetting any attempt at professional demeanor during our visit, the consulting physician looked at my son and incredulously blurted out, "That other doctor wants to do WHAT to that lovely little boy?"

In any case my son did wind up needing the surgery but that doctor's horror kept echoing in my mind all throughout the 6 hour surgical procedure serving to greatly compound my own already high anxiety.

Of course the candid often unprofessional approach of physicians' medical discussions with me was also extended to their often unprofessional discussions with my children. My son once went to an excellent dentist I had known for years, My son was a very bright independent young man and wanted to handle the first visit on his own while I waited outside which would have been fine except for the strange sense of humor and unusual bedside manner this particular dentist had. Unaware that my son was too nervous to appreciate things meant as jokes, the dentist apparently terrified my son. He started off the exam by initially holding the instruments upside down and quietly musing that he hoped that this time he could remember how to use them. He next told my son that he needed dental x-rays which were safe if done properly but that you had to absolutely precisely time the radiation exposure or this whole list of dreadful things could happen to you. He then said he hadn't used this machine before and pretended to be studying the x-ray manual at great length before eventually shrugging his shoulders and handing the obviously preprogrammed x-ray exposure button to a child waiting in the hall and telling him loudly enough for my now completely terrified son to hear, "When I count to three, push the button."

With their mommy as a physician, my sons' attitudes toward their doctors was embarrassingly fairly casual too. Once when my youngest had a high fever and hacking cough I suspected pneumonia but wanted one of my partners to take a listen to confirm my diagnosis. My partner was kind enough to say he'd stop by our house later that night on his way home.

With his illness my son was meanwhile finding bright lights very bothersome and so we were keeping his room dark. When my partner arrived at our house, my son feeling too ill to be able to muster up any concern for any difficulties this might cause the doctor coming to see him, continued to refuse to allow any lights on in his room or hall outside his room. Although a mother is familiar with every inch of her house, it's still hard for her to safely maneuver across a growing boy's toy packed room in broad daylight but for an outsider to safely cross a room full of Legos, books, balls, and race cars in total darkness can be quite a challenge After my partner groped across the room, located my son, and listened to his chest all in absolute darkness, he apologetically asked my son if he could use his small penlight otoscope to briefly check his ears and throat before leaving. Several days later when my son had recovered from the pneumonia, I mentioned to him that I thought it had been terribly rude and unfair of him to have made his doctor see him in total darkness. My son seemed surprised at my complaint and said that it hadn't been totally dark because after all my partner had had his tiny flashlight.

A Typical Day

OVER THE YEARS SEVERAL friends suggested that I describe a typical day as a mother-pediatrician. The concept alone is a joke since I never had a typical day in any of the years since starting my career but will try describing at least some of the events of a random day.

The so called typical day would actually have to start with a description of the night before. Parents often complained to me that their four month old baby still occasionally woke them during the night. Myself, I cannot recall sleeping through a single night ever since medical school. When I wasn't on call getting middle of the night phone calls then my husband would have been on call getting his middle of the night calls.

When we were both off call then one of our boys would have a nightmare or become ill during the night. If they were both well and neither of us on call, then one of the pets would act up. When our dog had been a puppy she'd attack our boys' stuffed animals at 2:00 am. Many nights we'd get awakened by her growling while being surrounded by flying cotton in the middle of a fierce battle with some poor stuffed giraffe or bear. When she became an older dog she stopped attacking the stuffed animals but would apparently have scary dreams and would suddenly leap up and stalk around snarling at her imagined ghosts.

The house itself had built-in wake up noises. Occasionally on a quiet night one of our smoke alarm batteries would weaken and start chirping the need for a new battery. This would wake us up and until realizing it had just been the battery, would have us all wide awake sniffing for smoke. Sometimes too we'd wake to hear a squirrel or some other critter running about in the attic or else a woodpecker attacking an outside wall so nights were very rarely fully quiet. Additionally our bedroom has a window air conditioner over the bed with accordion sides which unknown to us our cat had learned to open.

We thought he was an indoors only cat but he'd apparently had other ideas and one night we discovered to our surprise that while we were asleep he had been going outside each night through the air conditioner's accordion sides and returning the same way before we woke up. His escapes through the air conditioner were totally quiet as would have been his returns except that they involved a leap over the bed. In fact we would have never known about his secret escape route or outdoor escapades at all except for one night when it had been snowing very heavily. In the middle of the night in question he decided to return from his outside jaunt and as usual leap back in through the air conditioner. This time although still silent, his leap totally woke me up as the fresh snow shook off his fur onto my previously fast asleep face as he leapt over it.

Every night always had some sort of problem. On nights when the children, patients, dog, and cat were all sleeping peacefully, we'd often get a call from a neighbor that one of our horses had just been seen running through their vegetable garden. We had a large paddock that not only had a wooden fence but also had an electric wire on top but when the horses felt the urge to wander, off they'd go. Sometimes it would be to meet a horse who lived on the next street, sometimes it would be that the grass looked greener on the other side of the fence, and sometimes the reason for their escape was inexplicable and maybe had just seemed like a fun idea at the time because after these escapades they were always very affectionate when found and more than happy to be led back to the comfort of their own stall and yard.

As explained, no night was ever peaceful but some had stranger events than others. I distinctly still recall the memorable night when all the animals were settled down and my husband and I were off call and the whole household seemed peaceful. My younger son had been ill for several nights but had finally had a normal temp that evening and was resting comfortably so we too were finally relaxed and sleeping calmly.

For some unknown reason though, at 4:00 am he apparently woke up and decided to give us an update. He tiptoed quietly to the bathroom and then came into our room and woke us from our sound sleeps by announcing that he had come to let us know that he still felt fine and wanted to say goodnight. He then trundled off peacefully back to bed while we stayed sitting bolt upright, trying to understand why he had wakened us at 4:00 am simply to say goodnight.

Anyway, on the night prior to the particular sample day I'll describe, we had all gone to bed calmly, hoping to finally break our record of the longest number of consecutive sleepless nights. Fate had deemed otherwise though and once again 3:00 am found my husband and I sitting wide-eyed listening to the eerie sound of an animal trapped in our attic and gnawing at the ceiling beam directly over our heads. Needless to say, the thought of some creature chewing his way through the ceiling and falling directly onto the bed was enough to keep us awake for quite a while but eventually the noises finally stopped and we assumed whatever animal it had been had gotten back outside so fell back asleep.

The following morning my husband left for work at his usual 7:00 am as I tore through the house tossing a load of clothes in the washer, setting the table for dinner that night, and hurriedly packing school lunches prior to a 7:30 shower and getting ready for work. The horses were fed by 8:00 and breakfast ready for my son when the first cries of "I don't feel well" drifted down the stairs.

It's hard enough to find a kind, loving baby-sitter under ideal circumstances, but on one half hour notice and at 8:00 am it's close to impossible. I was dialing my last possible lady when the smell of dog droppings filled the house and I realized the hard way that in the morning chaos no one had let the dog out. Most dogs whine or scratch when they have to go out but ours used to sit quietly by the door patiently hoping to be noticed and on hectic mornings I'm embarrassed to say she was occasionally overlooked.

That was why all our living room plants had charcoal briquettes in their pots to absorb odor rather than as a clever fertilizer as some guests supposed. Anyway, I let the dog out and then tried to figure out how to handle both my patient load that day and my poor son who was feeling sick. There was no easy solution other than having my son who was too ill for school but not ill enough to have to stay in bed come spend the day with me at work. We packed a shopping bag full of toys and books and set of for my office. Once at the medical center my son settled down comfortably into my private office with his toys and juice and the cookies provided by our very sympathetic nurses and the day began.

Medical school had never discussed the days when you'd run from sore throat to earache to pneumonia to sore throat again, seeing two children every 15 minutes, all punctuated by phone calls from frantic parents and quick visits to one's own child for a hug, glass of juice and a kiss. Fortunately, the morning passed uneventfully although my son did ask me afterward why I had given a little girl a shot and made her cry.

At lunch time I was able to locate a sitter for my son and get him back home before returning to work. The afternoon had more frustrations and wildness however such as the parent who wanted her child seen that day but couldn't come at the offered squeezable times of 2:00, 2:30, 3:00, 3:45, 4:30 or 5:00 and then got angry that her ill child couldn't get an appointment to be seen that day.

There were also a number of children with actual ear infections plus one baby the mother bought in suspecting she might have an ear infection because the baby suddenly didn't seem to be hearing well. That child's ears turned out to be totally fine except for the multiple small beads I found and removed from each ear which her older sister eventually admitted to having carefully placed there while her baby sister had been sleeping.

There was also a 6 year old child who was brought in for an evaluation because his teacher had said he couldn't read but who turned out to actually be a very good reader and explained that he wouldn't read out loud in class because he didn't like his teacher so didn't want to read to her.

A final highlight was the mother who calmly continued her questions about toilet training either totally oblivious or else purposely choosing to ignore the fact that during the discussion her son had quietly walked over and given me a swift unprovoked kick in the shins. In any case the rest of the afternoon went smoothly and meanwhile I knew that my son was being well cared for at home.

It was flu season so there were many children needing to be seen making it a very busy stressful day but there were also several strikingly satisfying encounters that afternoon. These included an appointment with the beautiful bright now healthy little girl who several years earlier had had to undergo major cardiac surgery; the adorable outgoing inquisitive little boy who at birth had been a tiny sick premature infant, and the grateful formerly anorexic teenager who stopped by on an impulse just to bring me two long stemmed roses.

Between these extremes were a myriad of anxious parents, sick children, thriving babies and healthy youngsters all developing steadily into their own unique and wonderful people.

Office hours finished and final phone calls were made before leaving, beeper in hand, to pick up my older son at soccer practice. After eventually arriving home and feeding the animals I stood, coat still on, staring dismally at the refrigerator, wondering how to get the energy to create a dinner and all the while hearing a chorus of, "Come quick and look at the picture I made." "Can you figure out this math problem?" "Get him out of my room." And, "Come look what the dog did now." An hour later while struggling to help my son with his last math problem, it was a shock to hear my husband's car in the driveway and look at the clock as I sat with my coat still on and dinner still off.

The evening continued at the same frantic pace as I checked my son's temperature with one hand and held the phone with the other hand while dispensing medical advice to parents who had also just arrived home and discovered their child ill. Before bed I then played a last bedtime board game, tucked the boys in, let the dog out, checked on the horses, and then made my fourth revised list of the multiple office, home and barn chores which would have to be dealt with the following day.

My Husband

MY HUSBAND MARK IS wonderful, a special blend of the liberated male delighted that his wife had a career and male chauvinist who would have liked, but learned not to expect, dinner to be on the table promptly as soon as he arrived home. We actually shared that wish. We both grew up in middle class families where the mother did all the traditional cooking, cleaning, and catering to the children's demands. It was a shock after marriage, therefore, when we both looked around at 6:00 and waited for dinner to magically appear on the table.

Mark's support of my endeavors, however, was always terrific and punctuated by the constant great encouragement of, "You can do it." He listened patiently as I complained of exhaustion and the scores of phone calls to return, piles of wash to sort, and the mountains of manure to be moved. He would then reassure me that he was confident that I would manage it all well as I shouldered my shovel, and he sat down to turn on the TV news.

I recall the time I broke my leg horseback riding and was in a full toe-to-groin plaster cast. The first morning that I finally felt well enough to try a tub bath I gingerly lowered myself in, casted leg encased in plastic bags and resting on a hamper, as I heard my husband getting ready to leave for work. Not sure I could manage to climb out of the tub since I had never done it with such a weighted, useless limb, I called out that he should wait two minutes in case I needed him to help me. His concern was apparent as he called back that he was already late for work and had to go but that if I couldn't get out of the tub I should pull the plug to let the water out so I wouldn't drown and that the sitter could help me get out when she arrived in an hour.

My pride makes me digress here to let it be known that I didn't break my leg falling off my horse. It's a small point but important to my ego to stress that I broke my leg by purposely jumping off the horse when he got spooked by a dog and I was unable to control him as he raced right into traffic. My pride wants it clear that I didn't fall, but my mind does feel pretty stupid since the horse made it home perfectly safe and sound as I would have if I had not abandoned ship at a full gallop onto the concrete.

Anyway, the close relationship between my husband and myself was clear in our many activities together; tennis, skiing, hiking, dancing, riding. The bond was strained, however, at times of contrast with certain other couples we knew. My partner, for example, was a warm caring man with limitless devotion to his family. One day many years ago there was a scheduled town wide meeting to discuss elementary school budget problems. My partner and my husband had both planned to try to get home early so as to be able to attend. That day it began snowing very heavily and the meeting had to be postponed. I was intrigued as I sat talking with my partner when he answered the phone and I heard him saying, "Aren't you sweet; aren't you wonderful' that was so nice of you to do this."

He turned and explained that his enthusiastic praise was for the thoughtfulness of his wife who on hearing that a town hall meeting we had all been planning to attend had been called off due to the weather and thinking he shouldn't have to rush unnecessarily, had called to tell him about the meeting having been canceled After brief consideration I decided that my poor husband should also know that he didn't have to rush home so I called his hospital and had him paged. When he answered I sweetly conveyed the same message that had earned my partner's wife such glowing appreciation. My husband's response, however, was a prompt, "What! You paged me in the middle of the day just to tell me THAT?"

With both of us doctors my husband and I shared many common interests and were always able to have a clear understanding of each others career, concerns, worries and rewards. My husband's reaction was therefore a surprise when I came home late one night due to having had to work long hours over a critically ill child who came to the emergency room with a prolonged seizure. Although thrilled that the little girl was finally stable and in the ICU, I arrived home physically and mentally exhausted from the strain of trying to treat this severely ill youngster. By that time our sitter had long ago gone home and my usually sympathetic but now famished husband held our crying son over a pile of dirty diapers as he glared at me with a, "Why are you so late? Couldn't anyone else have helped that child?"

These events were extremely rare though and generally my husband took my worries as his worries, and over the years I developed a profound trust in him and his superb medical skills. I, however, neglected to realize that his medical judgments were much less brilliant when he was asleep. Some nights I'd stumble home after a late but routine hospital admission secure in the knowledge that my patient would be better by morning and so be almost asleep myself next to my already fast asleep husband, only to hear my sleeping and probably dreaming husband mumble, "Did you check his zinc level?"

This would make me sit up totally awake for hours, knowing intellectually that the zinc level had nothing whatsoever to do with my patient's illness but nonetheless feeling sure that my husband's sleepy mind had thought of a crucial test that I had overlooked, and that I should try to figure out what possible significance a zinc level could possibly have in this case.

All in all we managed to work out how to best handle the strains of our demanding careers and often conflicting schedules and our shared interests proved to be fertile ground for our marriage to grow stronger although our both having careers in medicine did make for dinner conversations considered pretty odd by our non-medical friends.

STORM CLOUDS

BEING MARRIED TO ME, my husband had to deal with lots of unique problems in addition to those caused by my also being a physician. With severe snowstorms or pending hurricanes my office would cancel routine appointments and close so that the nurses wouldn't have to drive on dangerous roads while having either myself or one of my partners on call from home and available to go meet any patients with urgent problems that could not wait. My husband however would always have to be at his hospital regardless of the weather. One memorable incident that really put my husband's patience to the test was a day in which he was at work and I was at home with a severe hurricane approaching our town.

The weather forecaster on the radio said it was going to be a huge storm with incredibly high winds so people should consider tying down their cars. We had gone through many storms before but I had never heard that particular odd piece of advice. Possibly the forecaster was kidding because I never did see any cars tied down but his words made me think that my horses might not weigh that much more than a car and so they might also need extra protection from the predicted dangerously high winds.

Our barn is a small simple structure with a large overhanging tree and the stall doors were always kept open to the field so that the horses could go in and out at will. Since the barn was so small and directly under a tree that might fall I wasn't sure that the horses would be any safer confined to the barn than out in the field where they currently were calmly grazing. Concerned however about the impending storm and the warning about cars, I called a local farmer to ask his advice since he was the person who delivered my hay and so knew my barn well. He agreed that I should not close the horses in the barn and told me that if the winds got really high the horses would just hold onto the wooden fence with their teeth. He added that if the winds got even higher and the trees began swaying dangerously that I could always go get them and put them in our basement since it had an entrance door at ground level and no stairs.

Our horses had been with us for years and I doubted that they'd know to hold onto the fence with their teeth having never seen them do anything like that in any previous storms. In any case they were also all older animals and so I worried that being old their teeth might not be strong enough to hold onto the fence anyway. I knew too that I'd find it terribly frightening to try catching the horses and moving them into the basement at the height of the storm so decided that I should do it before the storm started. I should add that our basement was a finished room with carpet and sofa and although large enough for all my animals, it was certainly not meant to house horses.

In any case, I opened the basement door wide and threw a bale of hay inside onto the carpet and then went to get the horses. The pony always followed me like a dog so she went willingly with me into the basement. One of the other horses also willingly followed me into the basement and promptly started calmly chomping the hay. When the other horse neared the basement door however, he took one look at the inside of the room, reared up, and in no uncertain terms make it clear that he would not step a single hoof onto that strange carpeted area no matter what, After many attempts of unsuccessful cajoling and prodding I eventually had to accept that it was a futile effort and so put all the horses back in the field to hopefully weather the storm in whatever ways nature intended.

Needless to say, when my poor husband came home from work and happened to go into the basement that night he was startled by seeing hay strewn all over the carpet. When questioned about it, I agreed that it was an unusual occurrence but told him that he was actually lucky to just have hay all over the place because what he could have found could have been much worse.

In any case the horses did manage to do fine through the storm as did we with the only casualties being the death of our tropical fish because the storm knocked out the power and we had no heat for five days. We felt bad about the fish dying but the tank did still look beautiful with its plants, tunnels, and bubblers and we worried about the safety of any possible new fish with future storms and inevitable power outages so for a long time we never replaced the fish we had lost. Friends would come over and still comment on our beautiful tank never noticing that there were no longer any fish in it.

As an aside, the hay in the basement actually turned out to be a good conditioning exercise for my husband when in later years we just had one rabbit and traveled with it in our small camper van. We kept the rabbit in a carrying case while we drove but when we stopped for the night we would let her out to freely hop all over the back of the van where we had our mattresses and camping gear.

The camping was fun and the rabbit seemed happy to be with us but she did have a temper and when released from the carrying case she'd express her anger at having been confined for so long during the drive by tossing her hay all over the place so that instead of us camping in a van with a rabbit, it was more like we were camping inside a rabbit cage. This was reminiscent of our hay covered basement although since she was a bunny and not a horse there was no threat of manure.

In any case, despite the storms, I loved living in New England with its changing seasons and never ceased being in awe of the gorgeous fall foliage and magical appearance of the sparkling snow but the Massachusetts weather did definitely pose difficulties for us as well as the horses. We had a long winding driveway to a garage under the house which we almost never used instead keeping our cars in front of the house and so more readily available for quick trips to the hospital or office. This was usually much more convenient but in winter did often result in our having to scrape windshields or push the cars off the ice. The estimated cost of plowing our long driveway was pretty steep though so each winter we put up with the aggravation but one year decided we had finally had enough and decided to use the garage and regardless of cost to hire someone to plow the driveway. This worked out really well until during one especially large snowstorm when our cars were in the garage and our plow person called to say that there was just too much snow this storm so he couldn't plow but would be happy to help us the next time. We were shocked and truly stuck since there were no other available plow people and no way we could shovel a drive that long by hand. Fortunately neither of us was on call for our patients that night but we would be the next day and had no idea how we'd ever get out until spring. Late that night though we suddenly saw flashing lights and heard clanging and banging and discovered that a kind neighbor with a plow had noticed our plight and "quietly" come to dig us out.

Sibling Rivalry

IN ADDITION TO THE challenges and rewards described earlier there were also many other very rewarding interactions. I distinctly recall one especially wonderful day. That was the day the little boy who had probably given me more bruised shins than any other patient I'd ever seen came dancing into the office and spontaneously gave me a huge hug and a kiss. It would have been easier to accept this as a sign of new affection if I hadn't recognized the fact that this was his first visit to the office with his new baby sister.

I'm sure his fear of having our relationship disrupted by this new arrival was at the root of his hug and also what led him to suddenly come over and give the baby a big kiss in the middle of my examining her. This was the same little boy who a few months before the infant's arrival had threatened that he would drop the new baby out the window and then run outside to watch her splat on the sidewalk. It's truly intriguing to watch the changes in many children after the arrival of a sister or brother and it is equally interesting to watch the reactions of the parents who often prefer to be blind to the dramas erupting about them.

One mother came to the office with her new baby and her three year old son and proceeded to tell me at great length about how much her son adored the baby and how he kissed and hugged her and smiled all day long. During this recital of beautiful sibling interactions, I observed her son to stealthily sneak over to the baby and try bending the baby's fingers backwards. When the mother noticed this and interrupted his tortures, he proceeded to pinch the baby's toe to the background music of his mother saying, "He doesn't have a jealous bone in his body and just cannot kiss her enough." Other times I was the one fooled by the behavior of children in the office. One little girl sat quietly on the examining room table next to her new little baby intently watching the exam and smiling at her infant sister while the mother and I spoke. Despite this loving scene the mother proceeded to tell me how the older sister could not accept having the baby in the house and was constantly making trouble and demanding attention. She expressed worries that the older sister might one day harm the baby. I tried to calmly discuss sibling reactions with the mother and reassured her that her daughter's behavior was quite normal. While talking I was lovingly beaming at the two adorable little girls who were constantly smiling at each other when suddenly without any warning the older sister took off her shoe and bashed the baby on the head.

Once children learn to accept that their new baby is a permanent part of the family, they usually do develop great love and concern though. I recall hearing the story from my own childhood that when I was an infant just a few months old, my older sister would stand next to my carriage and tell me how much she loved me and asking whether I loved her too. After obviously receiving no reply from my two month old self she was then heard to persist in trying to get an answer by saying, "Now I am your older sister, Barbara Sara Bessin. I know that you're too young to talk but if you love me please shake your head."

I also recall when older and sick with some kind of bug that the pediatrician came to the house to examine me and probably give me a shot of some sort like he usually did, my sister stood by the door with a baseball bat and threatened him that if he dared hurt her sister, she'd let him have it. Children I saw in the office were usually less threatening but no less concerned. One little boy used to get so upset to see his baby brother get a vaccination shot that he had to run out of the room and wait in the hall. On one occasion while he was waiting in the hall, he went so far as to try to understand why we were hurting the baby by analyzing the pros and cons with the receptionist and telling her that he guessed the shot was necessary, the good part being that the baby wouldn't get sick and the only bad part being getting the shot at all.

One four year old girl particularly stands out in my memory as she tried to figure out how to be a good "big sister" during her one year old brother's exam. She hovered over him throughout his visit cautioning me constantly not to hurt him because he was so very little. At the end of his exam, I explained to her that he was going to need a little blood test which might hurt for a second but that she could help by being very nice to him afterwards since he might be feeling sad. She solemnly said that she would be very nice to him and would give him hugs and kisses afterward but would it be okay with me if she covered her ears while he screamed.

A further advantage of having a sister or brother becomes clear to my patients early on in visits to the office when the older child would not only take one sticker as a reward for coming but would also stuff half a dozen more stickers into his pockets stating that they were for the baby, the baby's giraffe, the baby's teddy bear, and the baby's toy clown. One enterprising young boy, who was an only child, took a sticker after his exam and then asked his mother if she was pregnant. She told him that she wasn't, after which he persisted with a plaintive, "Are you sure?" His mother's definitive "Yes, I'm sure I'm not" met with a brief silence before he cheerily said, "Well, just in case..." as he stuffed an additional sticker for the possible future baby into his pocket.

AUTO ABUSE

FUNCTIONAL CARS ARE A necessity in this age of suburban living and especially so for doctors who must be able to count on getting to the office or hospital when called without first needing a tow truck. My husband and I, however, always had an inordinate amount of car troubles.

When living in a Boston apartment the main problem was theft. Despite several varieties of anti-theft contraptions our car was regularly "borrowed" by would-be joyriders and taken on excursions to the ocean. The drivers were never injured and also never found but we got frequent calls to claim our missing car from Cape Cod, the North Shore or Boston Harbor. It became such a common occurrence that one day after my husband had left for work and I was walking the dog past where we usually parked and noticed the car missing, I assumed it had been stolen, and notified our now familiar local police officer only to discover later that for some unknown reason my husband had decided that day to drive to work and so had taken the car himself.

After most of its adventures our car did eventually always turn up someplace safe and sound until the one final trip it made after which I was informed that it had run over a telephone pole. We took the news in stride since the car had had so many earlier strange disappearances and only later as my husband and I were going to the police garage to claim the car did we realize that its trips must now be over because to run over a telephone pole you must have had to first had to knock it down and that in doing that our small car would have suffered fatal wounds.

When we moved out of the city and with our additional space expanded our menagerie of creatures, our car was no longer stolen. It was however definitely abused as into our subcompact I stuffed children, dogs, bales of hay and hundred pound bags of grain. Needless to say the car's parts wore out often and we supported the local service station faithfully.

I also became an entertaining familiar neighborhood sight as I drove around town in my tiny rusted car with its windows all steamed up from my huge sheep dog who always stood on the back seat with his front paws on my shoulders while barking and salivating furiously.

When the time came for trading our car, the dealers noticed the claw marks, the slobber, the dog hair, the sprouting hay seeds on the floor carpeting, and the roar of the exhausted engine and announced their negligible trade in appraisal by sadly shaking their heads and murmuring in funereal tones that they were sure that we had spent many happy hours enjoying the car.

With our old car obviously worthless I decided to buy a new car and fell in love with a used one I passed on a used car lot near home. Unfortunately it had a manual transmission which I had no idea how to use. Hearing that mileage and traction would be better with a stick shift though, I decided to get it despite not knowing how to drive it figuring it couldn't be too hard to learn. The salesman gave me some quick instructions, handed me the keys, and watched anxiously as I bucked and lurched out of his yard onto the road to head to work.

Naturally, the car was sold without gas so my first stop had to be a gas station on the right hand side of the road. The attendant admired the car as he filled the tank and asked how the gears worked and whether or not I had to downshift on left turns. When I told him that I had no idea whether or not I did since I'd never made a left turn, he looked curiously at me, then at the mileage counter, and then wondered aloud to a friend nearby how on earth I had managed to drive 20,000 miles without ever turning left. He didn't realize how close his assumption of my somehow having never turned left was to the future truth. Try as

I might it was months until I was able to start the car without stalling and bucking and stalling again and so I became terrified of stop signs and left hand turns across traffic. My gas mileage was fantastic but my operating costs were high as I drove many extra miles out of my way to avoid traffic lights and left turns over the months that it took me to learn how to drive.

Turns and stops were not my only problems in this learning period as I also encountered the frustration of conquering hills with a manual transmission. On one memorable trip up a small hill I stalled and was totally unable to restart the car without rolling backwards or stalling again. This was a busy street and the line of traffic behind me kept growing longer. Suddenly, a wonderful policeman appeared asking if I was having car trouble. I told him that I thought the car was fine but that it was me having trouble, and that I'd probably be able to manage things if he could just please get in and drive me to the top of the hill. He never questioned the foolishness of the situation, never asked for my driver's license or even the car registration and instead patiently drove me to the top of the hill, got out, waved good-bye, and walked back to his car waiting at the bottom.

There were other car problems in addition to those of hills and left turns. One night we accidentally drove the 45 minute trip home from the hospital in second gear the whole way. My husband and I were engrossed in conversation when we suddenly became aware of an unexpected growing fog all around us. We drove along amazed at the suddenness and thick density of the fog until we finally came to realize that it was not a weather phenomenon at all and was instead our own personal fog from our badly overheated car.

Over time the car and I eventually reached an understanding and we had many wonderful trips around town until years later when it suddenly decided to spontaneously drop its muffler as I was leaving the hospital parking lot resulting in my roaring out like a young hot rodder. After strewing several other essential parts on several other main roads on subsequent travels it became clear that the car needed replacement.

My next car was well chosen for its durability, gas mileage and carrying capacity but it, too, had a difficult beginning. Shortly after purchasing the car I had a late night call to rush see a child having a seizure. I raced out of bed, threw on my clothes and tore off to the hospital in my brand new car getting there in record time. On arrival I became frantic as I unsuccessfully groped around in the dark for the new style recessed door handles. Unable to figure out how to open the doors I began to seriously contemplate breaking a window until I finally managed to find a light switch and successfully open the door.

MOVING DOOR-TO-DOOR

PHYSICIANS IN TRAINING USUALLY move around a great deal. College may be in one state, medical school in another, internship and residencies some other place and eventual practice elsewhere. In fact, my husband and I occupied five different apartments or houses in the first seven years of our marriage. Our very first apartment was a true find. Having very little money we managed to argue the landlord down from $140 a month to $135 and only half listened to his "no pets allowed" as we signed the agreement thinking the no pets sentence must be a joke since we had seen a lady with a dog in the model apartment he had shown us but when we moved in with our puppy, kitten, parakeet and tropical fish, he was shocked. He was further horrified when we also took in a guinea pig as a temporary boarder for a friend going on vacation.

It turned out that we were able to stay despite our zoo of animals though by virtue of the happy fact that the landlord was terrified of dogs. Every time he came to the door to tell us that the pets had to leave or else we did, the dog would run to greet him with her tail wagging and tongue rolling. He would take one frightened look at her and yell to forget it as he slammed the door and ran. Despite the bargain rental and because of our dog having no fear of the landlord evicting us, it soon became clear that we needed more space and should move.

Moving isn't simple though and like all subsequent moves, this one had many complications and problems. These ranged from trying to study despite the fact that one's spouse had packed an essential textbook in one of 15 unmarked cartons, to coming home late after a long day at the hospital and trying to move the furniture at that hour quietly enough so as to not wake the neighbors. With one of our moves there was the added problem of discovering on the day of arrival at our new apartment that the budget moving company we had hired which had advertised "door to door" delivery had literally meant just "door to door" and planned to leave the heavy furniture outside in the rain at the ground level door of the apartment building instead of carrying it upstairs to our third floor walkup door. We unsuccessfully pleaded with the movers to carry the sofa upstairs as we explained to them that our neighbors, though willing to help, were all over 80 years old. Finally, we had to call an additional second moving company to come meet the first company and then pay that second company for the "new move" from the ground floor to the apartment upstairs.

These had all been local moves so we had been dreading what would happen with our move out of state but were pleasantly surprised to find that our move from Massachusetts to Maryland actually went fairly smoothly. However, once arrived, my husband and I refused to believe that our new house had smaller rooms than our Boston apartment. On three separate occasions we stubbornly persisted in carrying the heavy rolled rugs up from the basement as we tripped on the stairs and banged into walls only to discover each time that the rooms had still not grown any bigger and that the rugs were still just too large. We finally became convinced that houses don't grow or shrink but the movers taking us back to Massachusetts two years later did not share that knowledge.

After several fruitless attempts to carry our refrigerator out of the kitchen they announced that there was no way the refrigerator could fit out the doors and that the room must have been altered or built around the refrigerator. This news was startling enough since the refrigerator had come into the house with us on our move down but due to their latest attempt we had the added trauma of now having our refrigerator securely wedged in the doorway meaning we could either eat cold food directly in the dining room or climb through a window to get to the stove. Somehow by finally taking the refrigerator apart we were eventually able to get it onto the moving van.

The only other delay on that trip was the time spent by the moving men in studying our bicycles. My dad was a great lover of gadgets and contraptions and had given us gifts of bicycles that could fold up to readily fit in the trunk of a car. As we paid by the hour the movers were fascinated as they folded and unfolded and refolded the bicycles.

Further moving troubles had nothing to do with the movers and involved arriving at our new homes and realizing that each house had some strange unexpected quirk of personality. There was the house in Maryland where at 4:00 am the overhead bedroom light would suddenly flash on for no apparent reason totally startling us out of any further possible sleep. We never discovered the reason for the occasionally flashing light but equally troubling was that that house also had a weak basement window latch.

Since our backyard and that of our neighbors all sloped down toward that window, the result of that poorly latched window was that on rainy nights torrents of water would run across our yard , force the window open and pour into the basement. During one heavy rainstorm the flood of water was as forceful as a sewer pipe. This resulted in our landlord doing the math calculations taught in high school to estimate that if the water entered a square container sized X or Y at a rate of R gallons per minute and there were T minutes left until morning, that the water level at 7:00 am might only be at the fifth basement step and so we could go back to bed on the first floor knowing that we wouldn't drown in our sleep.

We were delighted to leave that house behind when we moved back to Massachusetts. Our rented house in Boston was lovely with a nice back yard but a totally different water problem. The clothes washer and dryer were in the basement near an ample sized laundry sink and we had assumed that the sink and washer worked normally but after moving in it turned out we were very wrong. Unknown to us when we rented the house, the sink had no functional drain at all. To drain the water it was necessary to plug in a small floor pump which forced the water upstairs to a normal drainage system. The pump would burn out if run without water and the sink would flood the basement if used without the pump. Washing clothes therefore provided wonderful cardiovascular fitness exercise as well as auditory discrimination practice. I'd go down to the basement to put the clothes in the machine and turn it on before going back upstairs to study. At the first sound of water discharging from the machine into the sink I'd have to run downstairs to plug in the pump and return upstairs. As soon as the pump sounded dry I'd have to race downstairs again to unplug it before it burned and go back upstairs to listen for the rinse cycle at which time the whole exercise had to be repeated. It was too cold, damp, and noisy to stay in the basement throughout this whole operation so I'd study at the top of the stairs listening for the telltale sounds which would send me flying into action.

See One, Do One, Teach One

IN ADDITION TO DEALING with the family, animals, cars, and houses, there was always time needed for studying. In addition to providing direct patient care, being in medicine requires constant reading, refresher courses and teaching commitments in order to stay knowledgeable and maintain a license. Physicians at each level of training become the teachers of the next lower level. Interns teach medical students; residents teach interns; practicing staff teach residents and specialists teach staff. It is often expressed that in learning medical procedures at a busy hospital one must first see one, then do one, and then teach one.

Participating in each of these stages can be rewarding and challenging. Some of the experiences, however, were more memorable than others. I remember one brilliant instructor who unfortunately had an illness called narcolepsy. This is a disorder in which the person frequently suddenly falls asleep briefly but at random odd times.

Many a time one of my classmates or myself would be discussing a case only to glance over and notice that our instructor was sound asleep. We were never sure whether to wake him and thereby embarrass him, to stop talking and sit quietly while he slept, or to pass the time by continuing to talk about random topics to the now snoring teacher.

As a medical student I also clearly recall an overworked, zealous intern who took his teaching responsibilities extremely seriously. Many nights when we were on call together the activities of running the ward and admitting new patients kept us busy until well after midnight. Often at 2:00 am, my intern would suddenly realize that he had failed to keep his promise to teach me about EKG's or some other topic and would wake me up to hold an informal class on the subject. What I mainly learned in those midnight marathons was how to exist on minimal sleep and still sound coherent the next day.

I hope that the sessions I spent teaching interns and residents were better received. Most of the time the house staff I worked with were bright and enthusiastic. I do recall one physician in training, however, who has hopefully not continued in medicine. Our sessions together were unique as well as frustrating. When he was asked to discuss an ill child admitted for care from the emergency room his approach was definitely casual. When asked the age of the youngster he'd shrug and say, "Oh, he was a wee little tyke." This precisely aged the child anywhere from a premature infant to a short teenager.

When asked what the child's problem was, he'd say, "Oh, he was feeling pretty sick, all right." When asked how long the child had been ill he'd shrug again and say, "Who can say? I think he was sick quite a while." When I would finally be able to squeeze out of him a clear history and physical exam report, I was able to determine that the child was two and a half years old with a sudden onset of severe breathing difficulties which we diagnosed as croup.

The best was yet to come though as I then asked him to explain what croup was. He beamed and looked sure of approval as he said that he absolutely knew what it was because he had learned about it in medical school and clearly remembered the definition as being that croup was, "a diagnosis you could not afford to miss." When I realized that that was the full extent of all he knew that would define it I wondered how that piece of knowledge would ever help him to distinguish croup from meningitis, coma, diabetes or any other serious illness.

Further discussions with him about other topics proved equally rewarding. I recall one session where he actually questioned the entire germ theory of infectious disease by emphatically stating that he couldn't believe that a germ which was unable to thrive on its own outside the human body would ever actually harm or kill its human host and thereby itself.

Most of the other house staff I encountered however were fun to work with, dedicated, and extremely knowledgeable adding as much to my education as I tried to give to theirs. In addition, there were frequent informative staff lectures and refresher courses to attend. I clearly recall, however, one memorable CPR recertification course. Cardiopulmonary resuscitation, CPR, is a crucial skill to have and one that is taught in medical school and clearly necessary to know when working in the hospital. As a practicing physician it is less often necessary but recertification courses are taken regularly to stay familiar with the techniques anyway just in case. This particular class had been advertised as a quick refresher for the busy practitioner and my partner and I went to take it together one evening.

Once there it became clear that the instructor was aiming the class at beginners and also running it like an army drill sergeant. We had to practice resuscitating this air-filled plastic dummy over and over and over again as the instructor watched and our lips got blistered from the repeated mouth to mouth breathing on the hard plastic. Each practice resuscitation had to start with asking the dummy, "Are you all right? Are you all right?" If you did the whole procedure correctly but that initial question was forgotten you had to start all over again.

My partner and I became increasingly frustrated as the hour got later and later and we sat through person after person's practice attempts at resuscitation. Finally, three hours later, after the umpteenth sample resuscitation of the dummy, it was my partner's turn again. He started by leaning over the plastic dummy and asking, "Are you all right? Are you all right?" like all of us had been taught to do. He then stood up and told the instructor that the dummy said she was fine now so we could all go home.

LIFE IS FULL OF SURPRISES

THERE WERE A NUMBER of startling events during my time in practice but the most embarrassing one happened totally out of the blue one weekend far from the office. As in all doctor's offices, pharmaceutical representatives would stop by the office from time to time in order to introduce us to new medications and leave samples of over the counter medicines, formulas, or diapers for patients unable to afford them. The weekend I'm recalling was one in which my husband had signed up to run a mini marathon in RI.

The night before the race we were strolling around in a room that was selling all sorts of vitamins and health foods. The place was crowded with runners and other health conscious people when all of a sudden the pharmaceutical man who used to come to our office spotted me and called out loudly all across the room, "I know you, I used to sell you drugs."

A less embarrassing but still very startling event involved a former patient who on graduating from our pediatric practice to an internist had been wished luck and told that we would always still be there for him anytime he might need help in the future. We of course had assumed he would know we meant help with any medical concerns so were astounded when almost 10 years later he called to remind us of the offer and asked if we could help him with the down payment for a car.

A further startling event worth mentioning was the time a parent called requesting a prescription for a swimming pool. She said that her child was asthmatic as we knew and that everything she had read said that exercise was good for asthmatics. She added that since swimming was known to be one of the best forms of exercise she wanted us to write a prescription for a backyard pool so that her insurance would cover its installation. When over the shock at hearing such an amazing request I was able to remind her that there was a YMCA with a pool in the very next town.

In addition to the examples above, some of the most surprising events were the parents who had been extremely worried about their child possibly having some terrible disease but would then be upset after having made the trip to the office or hospital ER and discovered once there that their child actually wasn't critically ill at all. One such episode that stands out in my mind was a mother who called because she was worried about her daughter who was suddenly very lethargic, running a high fever, and complaining of a stiff neck and severe headache. She was told that her child needed to be seen right away because these were worrisome signs of possible meningitis.

The mother said she was in the middle of a dinner party and asked if the visit could wait several hours until her guests had all gone home. She was told meningitis could be quickly fatal so had to be ruled in or out immediately and that there was no way to do that over the phone. When in the ER and the LP and other tests had shown that her daughter had a severe strep throat and not meningitis, the mother was furious since she had had to leave her guests for "nothing."

Of course there were also always parents who wanted their children seen immediately no matter what. One memorable such visit was for a child whose mother called saying she needed an urgent visit that same day because her son was having terrible stomachaches. I squeezed her son in by completely rearranging my otherwise packed schedule but when the child arrived he was playful and in absolutely no distress at all. When I asked the mother why she had felt the visit was needed so urgently that day when her child was clearly feeling pretty well, she replied that he had complained of stomachaches on and off for his whole life and when that morning he had once again mentioned having a stomachache her husband had said he just couldn't stand hearing about it for one more second.

SORRY, WRONG NUMBER

OFFICE PEDIATRICS WAS EXTREMELY busy with me sometimes needing to see 30 children a day but just as demanding were the frequent phone calls. In fact so much of a pediatrician's time is spent on the phone that I often felt as if it was a permanent part of my face. While struggling to examine a fearful youngster I used to muse that God must have never been a pediatrician or else He'd have given children one large ear in the middle of their forehead. Now I think that God put ears on the side of the head because He must have known that it might be necessary for doctors to balance a phone on one shoulder while stirring spaghetti sauce, sewing a button, or finding homework papers with the other arm.

There were so many medical calls when my husband and I got home from work and were even off duty that we decided to try a phone answering machine. We initially used the message, "We're sorry, we're not home at the moment but if you leave your name and number at the tone, personal calls will be returned as soon as possible. To discuss medical problems, please call the office number to reach the doctor who is on call today."

Our very first message was a male voice saying, "Since you're not home at the moment, I'll be right over to rob your house." We recognized the caller as my partner but realized the obvious need to change the message.

Of course it wasn't only medical calls which invaded our privacy. Some nights after spending hours at the office talking, talking, talking, it became hard to want to talk to anyone else, whether in person or even on the phone. Those were usually the nights that a rug cleaning company would call with an introductory offer; a magazine subscription service would call with an exciting new deal; a telephone contest would call with a coupon book for telling them who was buried in Grant's Tomb; a stockbroker would call with a surefire way to get rich overnight, or some other telemarketer or scam caller.

Having forgotten to turn on the answering machine we would hear the phone ring and ring and ring as my husband and I looked at each other saying, "You get it."

"No, you get it."

"No, you get it, it must be for you."

Eventually one of our sons would answer only to find that the caller had given up and was gone.

As soon as portable phones and cell phones became available my parents decided to make life a little easier for us and sent us one as a gift. This was great. I could now take calls easily from the barn or from the bathtub. The phone even had a re-dial feature with which, if the number you wanted was busy, you could just push a button and the phone would automatically re-dial.

Unfortunately, our phone had a mind of its own. On Father's Day I tried calling my dad and had to use the re-dial feature. After many tries I eventually reached a man in my parents' home town who sounded unfamiliar but was absolutely delighted to hear from me. I said he sounded strange and asked if he was really my father? He said of course he was and that my voice sounded strange over the phone too but that he had just been thinking of me and was so glad I had called all the way from Florida. This confirmed my earlier suspicion that I had in fact reached the wrong father. He sounded so lonely, however, that it was a hard decision whether to disappoint him by truthfully telling him I had reached the wrong number or whether to continue to talk with him pretending to be his daughter from Florida.

The problems with the telephone were mild though when compared to the situations which arose with the office answering service. The answering service had the enormous job of taking messages for several doctors' offices, plumbers, electricians, carpenters, and other businesses. In general they did a wonderful job but did have occasional lapses. For example, late one night they gave me the message that someone had called wanting to know what to do with a child who refused to go to bed and had been screaming for the last hour. The message was initially given very professionally but then the answering service lady added to it by muttering to me angrily under her breath, "I'm no doctor but I could tell her what to do with him!"

Once a parent calling was so distraught that she left our office number as the number where she could be reached. Neither the answering service nor I recognized the number so I spent a frustrating half hour calling myself and constantly getting a busy signal.

Another classic mix-up occurred the day the answering service beeped my partner with an urgent message that someone was anxious to know whether or not it was possible to have a delivery two weeks early. This seemed a somewhat reasonable question for a pediatrician until the rest of the message was added saying that the delivery was needed early since they had run out of towels. Obviously, the message had been meant for a laundry service and somewhere there was probably the driver of a laundry truck wondering what to tell the woman whose child had just swallowed a button.

Other nights the answering service mix-ups were even more frustrating. One night the service called at 3 am waking me from a sound sleep and then proceeding to give me a long list of urgent messages. I resigned myself to another long wakeful night as I rummaged about for a flashlight, pad and pencil. Only after having woken my husband with my hunting around for a pencil and after having finished copying down the last of the several phone numbers on the list did the answering service person suddenly say, "Whoops! These messages are for a different medical group. You're all clear."

RELATIVE ROOTS

NO BOOK ABOUT LIFE can be complete without a chapter about families, mothers, and mothers-in-law. At least I certainly hope that my remembering to include my mother and mother-in-law will encourage my sons, now grown, to always remember to include me. Also my family was always a major source of strength and inspiration to me and so definitely deserves mention as a large support factor in helping me juggle home and career.

I only hope that I will always have the kind of energy and enthusiasm that made my grandmother, father and mother always such fun to be with. My grandmother, for example, took a train trip out west with friends when she was in her late eighties and complained afterward that there had been nothing to do at night because the "old people" would all go to bed early.

My mother, who swam her age in laps daily even in her 80's once signed up for an aerobics class where her age was the sum of the ages of the other four women in the group. In addition to being incredibly energetic, my mother was a wonderful, loving person and generous to a fault. If I admired her skirt, she'd take it off and say she had actually bought it for me. If I admired her sweater, I'd find one just like it in the mail the next week. If while having dinner at her house I'd compliment her vegetables, she would arrive on her next visit from NY to Boston with a carton of New York supermarket canned vegetables as if Boston was an outpost of Siberia.

I once mentioned needing a desk and totally unknown to me, my dad, or anyone else, she left New York after breakfast, drove my childhood desk the five hours to Boston, persuaded the landlord to bring it upstairs into our apartment so that it would be there when we came home from work and then left driving home to New York that same day in time to make dinner for my dad and casually tell him about her day. Despite all her good deeds, however, my husband will probably most remember her visit after our first son was born.

We had been happily married for over three years when our child was born and my mother came to help. The first night home from the hospital my newborn son fussed and cried a lot while my mother and I took turns pacing the floor with him. My mother who, as I said, had many wonderful attributes, unfortunately could not carry a tune. My husband had been up all night with a patient the previous night and as he lay in bed exhausted he was unable to sleep as he listened to the wailing of his baby, the moaning of his wife and the off-key crooning of his mother-in-law while wondering if it was too late to forget the whole business and return to the life of being single back in the dorm.

My mother-in-law was also a charming helpful person. She was very generous although she did once get angry at my husband who was devouring an entire fruit basket at one sitting. Without thinking she criticized him with the statement that he shouldn't eat so much fruit because, after all, fruit didn't grow on trees.

She was a marvelous cook though and her generous holiday shipments of home-baked goods was always so huge that it completely filled our freezer so that we often barely had any room for meat or vegetables. She, however, had a fetish about cleanliness. When first married I used to scrub the house in preparation for her visits. Nonetheless she would invariably arrive, take off her coat, look about and say, "I can tell you've been busy working and haven't had time to clean so let me help you," as she'd then re-vacuum where I had just vacuumed and re-dust where I had just dusted.

Once before one of her visits I made a private game of spending my entire day off scouring the house before she would come. She arrived and as usual asked for a dust cloth. I was inwardly grinning as I handed her a spanking white cloth mentally daring her to find one speck of dirt. I was shocked when she returned a short while later with a filthy cloth saying, "You should remember to clean inside the cabinets and also dust the screen of that television inside the living room cupboard." After that her visits became less stressful for me because I stopped cleaning at all before her arrival since I knew she'd redo it anyway.

On the other hand my husband and I must have made her life crazy too because when we'd visit her in Illinois we'd always bring our dog. My in-laws' house was lovely and neat and had never before had a furry creature step across the threshold. In fact, unknown to me, no living creature of any sort including human had ever entered the all white living room with the plastic covered furniture.

I was unused to the concept of a living room not being lived in so on our first arrival after a long harrowing plane ride with our dog, I promptly took off my shoes and plunked down on the white sofa confused at what I could have possibly done wrong as I saw my mother-in-law watching from the doorway with mingled surprise and horror. She was, however, a marvelous sport and never once complained about us or the dog as she silently tried to be inconspicuous while cautiously following the dog from room to room with a damp mop all weekend. The dog, who actually was still a puppy and only barely housebroken, somehow managed to stay out of trouble and be absolutely charming so that after we left my in-laws eventually decided to get a dog of their own.

My father-in-law was a warm sensitive man who was always a pal to his grandchildren and patiently played hours of games with the boys and once even bravely took them fishing even though it turned out he had never fished a day in his life before and so had no idea how to bait the hook. It was immaterial that he also did not know how to remove a fish since he and the boys had a great day but caught only seaweed.

My own dad was the life of the party and always able to recall a good joke or see the wacky humor in a situation. He was also loving and generous to a fault giving his children and grandchildren the best of whatever they wanted and was always proud of whatever they did whether it was in the classroom or on the ball field. He also had an unquenchable thirst for knowledge and drive for accomplishment. As a child if he got back a test with a 98 he'd retake it to try to get 100. Once when my son claimed to hate math, my dad started thinking up all sorts of intriguing math puzzles so that soon my son was begging for more number games and wanting to play multiplication instead of geography on our family drives. My dad's other passion was for gadgets and when his closets were full he'd send some to us.

Our house was quickly overrun by the clever but rarely used machine that automatically peels apples into long skinny strips, the fake gun that fires quarters at tollbooths, the indoor hose for watering plants, the underground doggy septic system, the mechanized children's toys that move on voice commands, the folding bicycles, and a lamp that lights when you touch it. This lamp was useful and very clever but proved a fascinating new source of midnight wakenings as it mysteriously turned itself on and off at strange hours. We accused the dog of touching it, a wind of blowing it, and even began to think the house was haunted until we finally discovered that its sensitivity was such that it was detecting the currents in the fish tank and turning itself on and off with the pump.

WHEN I GROW UP

PEDIATRICS CERTAINLY HAD ITS stressful moments but it was also very rewarding and an incredible privilege to be able to be part of so many different familys' lives and over time be able to watch their children grow and then bring their own children to the office for me to be able to watch them grow as well.

One of the other delights of pediatrics was rediscovering children's unique sensibilities and literal perspectives often forgotten by many adults. I always tried to engage my patients of all ages in conversations and would always ask the older ones about their activities and interests mainly to gain their trust and help make them feel more comfortable during their exams but also because I simply enjoyed getting to learn more about them. Although constantly talking with children, I would still sometimes be surprised by what some would say or their reactions to things I would say.

It was easier to connect with some patients than with others and some conversations were easily forgotten afterward but many were quite memorable. One example is the 5 year old little boy had recently had a class trip to the Aquarium and came to the office still bubbling over with excitement about the sharks, jellyfish, eels, and dolphins. I mentioned to him that with his obvious interest he might want to be a marine biologist when he grew up. He sounded intrigued and asked me what marine biologists did. When I told him that they were scientists who studied the creatures who lived in the ocean, he looked at me with disdain and said, "why on earth would I want to do that? I already know all about them."

One day a mother brought her three year old to see me because he had a fever and congestion. Stooping to floor level so that I could talk to him eye-to-eye as he clutched his mother's leg, I sympathized with his feeling sick and asked him if anything in particular bothered him. Expecting the usual response of "my ear" or "my tummy", I was caught by surprise when he hesitated briefly and then softly whispered "squirrels." This was naturally of no help in diagnosing his current illness but I was pleased that he had felt trusting enough to share with me what I later learned was a secret terror of his.

Another child came for a general checkup and after the usual questions about her activities, appetite, etc., I asked the open-ended question, "Did you have any particular worries to discuss today?" only to get the sincere response, "Yes, I've been worried all day about coming here and maybe getting a shot."

Children are often very helpful in describing their symptoms as they solemnly tell me that they have a "bug" in their ear or a "war" in their tummy, or that the "purple stuff" tastes great but isn't helping them and so they think they need the "bubble gum stuff" instead. Some children, in fact, outdo themselves in trying to cooperate fully. One little 3 year old came to see me with a complaint of a persistent cough. He was a serious little boy who earnestly tried to be as helpful as possible during my exam. After examining his throat, ears, and neck and after listening to his chest, I asked him to give a cough.

We stood in silence for a few moments before he stated sadly that he was trying but couldn't cough. I asked him to just try once more for even a tiny fake cough. He quietly stood there a few more moments before solemnly stating that he just couldn't cough but that if I wanted him to, he could probably "frow up."

Other children try to be helpful in other ways and minimize their problems. An example was the little girl I saw who had a fever and running nose. As I examined her, I asked her if she had sore ears. She smilingly said, "only two of them."

Some poor children are constantly sick and therefore very knowledgeable about office procedures, the various medicines and how soon they'll feel better but some luckier ones are almost never ill and so find their sudden pains or fevers very frightening. One little girl had her first ear infection at age four and had come to the office crying with pain and fear. Throughout my exam she kept anxiously repeating that her ear still hurt and telling her mother that seeing the doctor wasn't helping at all. When I handed her the prescription I told her that if she went with her mommy to the drug store, the pharmacist there would give her some yummy medicine in exchange for the piece of paper and that the medicine would make her ear feel all better. Her sense of hopelessness vanished and her delight was evident as she suddenly brightened and announced "That's a great idea."

Most of my patients enjoyed coming to the doctor's office since they enjoyed having a fuss made over them and they liked going home with a sticker. One mother, however, recalling her own bad childhood medical experiences, tried to be consoling and sympathetic while driving her young daughter to the office and so had asked her, "Are you afraid?" The little girl promptly said "no" and then quizzically asked her mother, "Are you afraid?" The mother also said "No." The child had apparently thought quietly for a while and then asked her mother, "Do you think the doctor is afraid?"

The stickers we gave the children after their exams came to the office in bulk with no choice on our part as to design. Most popular were the rabbits with bandaged ears saying, "I have an earache", the elephants with a Band-Aid saying, "I was shot", the weird little insect saying, "I caught the flu bug", and the Ninja turtles and Barney stickers. Mixed in with these was an occasional valentine sticker saying, "I love my pediatrician." This last sticker was not very popular and most kids only picked it if the others were all gone. One day, however, a little boy quickly picked the "I love my pediatrician" sticker and proudly showed it to his mother. It made me really happy he had chosen it until I overheard him ask her, "But what's a pediatrician?"

There was clearly a lot of fun in dealing with children but frustrations did abound in pediatrics in ways very different than when caring for adults. An example is the time I tried to return a parent's call only to have her young son answer the phone and tell me abruptly before hanging up on me that his mommy was home but had told him to say that she couldn't come to the phone because she was waiting for an important call from the doctor.

Nonetheless even after having been in practice for over thirty years, I still found the children so much fun to work with and so rewarding to treat that it made it easy to answer the little boy who looked up at me with big earnest eyes one day as he asked me the same question undoubtedly often asked of him, "And what do you want to be when you grow up?" His mother laughed and explained that I was already grown up and had decided to be his doctor. That was obviously true but I think we're all always growing and hopefully open to new adventures so I told him that it was actually a very good question that I was still working on. In fact it's actually a question that even now at age 77 I still think about today.

THE NEXT CHAPTER

I WAS IN PRACTICE FOR over 36 years and over that time had seen my earliest patients grow into adults with families of their own and I had begun caring for many of their children too. Over the years I had also become quite close with our nurses and other office staff. It was a hard decision therefore to retire and leave behind these people and the families whom I'd known for so long but I needed to be free to travel in order to help my own family. One of my sons had moved to NC and my husband and I wanted to be able to spend time with him, his wife, and our grandchildren plus my 96 year old mother in NY had become quite ill and I needed to spend more time with her. I therefore sadly said goodbye to my staff, took down my dusty old diplomas, and entered my new phase of life.

My medical knowledge did not go to waste though as countless friends and relatives continued to call wanting advice about their own illnesses or those of their children or grandchildren. I was always glad to help and it was actually wonderful to still feel needed but some days the phone rang so often that life seemed busier than when working.

Meanwhile my love of animals led me to become very active in various animal rights groups even becoming chairman of the board of one. I'm passionate and very serious about wanting to protect animals from cruelty but sometimes my animal protection activities can be fairly comical such as when a local TV station wanted to interview me about some exceedingly cruel monkey research I was protesting and asked if while doing the interview they could film me with my monkey. Needless to say they had to settle for pictures of me with my dog since despite the otherwise large menagerie of animals at my house, I did not have a monkey.

Retirement also gave me a lot more time to spend with my children and grandchildren. Every interaction was wonderful and cherished but some underscored more than others the fact that I was getting older. One example was my then 5 year old grandson suddenly asking me in the middle of a board game what was wrong with my face. When I asked him to explain what he was talking about, he said he was wondering what those lines were that were on my face.

Unfortunately the lines weren't the erasable magic marker type lines I had sometimes seen on my patients but were instead the permanent wrinkles of aging. Another such moment was the time I was in NC playing tennis with my grandchildren. I was in my 60's and feeling energized and healthy while bashing the ball around like a teenager when all of a sudden my then 3 year old grandson turned to me and totally out of the blue announced to me that I was going to die soon. I was pretty startled but trying to stay calm I asked him why he had said that to which he replied, "Because you're very very old." Those comments stay with me but were fortunately rare since my husband and I continued keeping up with the kids going with them on bike rides and hikes, playing lots of board games, tennis and bocce with them, and currently since they're older, also golf.

Our granddaughter was born on Halloween and every birthday party was a costume party and being kids at heart, my husband and I always dressed up too. Over the years we were clowns, Native Americans and various animals among other things. The most memorable time though was the time we were celebrating her 10th birthday at Disney World. My son told me that everyone got dressed in costume at Disney on October 31 so my husband and I met them at the park dressed as gigantic crayons. He was blue and I was yellow. Unfortunately my son had had his information wrong and although people might have worn costumes that night, during the day we were the only adults in costume. We had no other clothes with us at the park so were forced to spend the whole day as crayons . People thought we were part of the entertainment and came over wanting to take pictures with us and at one event meant just for children the host called out that in addition to the children coming to the stage, he also wanted the yellow writing utensil to come on up.

Many wonderful family interactions occurred over the years before and after that day and I couldn't be prouder of my sons, daughter-in-law, and grandchildren who are all wonderful bright sensitive creative thoughtful people who fortunately all also have great senses of humor which had clearly been passed down through the generations. One final episode though needs to be mentioned before ending this book. It happened when my middle grandchild was roughly about 6 years old and was playing the basketball game 21 in his driveway with my husband. In that game you have to take turns standing on a certain spot, try to make a basket, catch the rebound if you miss and try to make a basket from the place where you caught it.

My grandson hated to lose and my husband who was obviously older and bigger and therefore much better at the game hated to let our grandson win so emotions were high leading me to decide to join the game. I missed most of my shots, sometimes on purpose and other times just because I couldn't do them. My grandson who had been upset at constantly losing was starting to feel better because he was finally beating someone. After several minutes of playing I said to my grandson that I guessed I just wasn't too good at basketball. Being a sweet sensitive boy then as now, he wanted to make me feel better so immediately said what was probably the first positive thing he could think of and said, "but you're very good at one thing." I asked him what that was, hoping to hear something about my being a wonderful grandmother, giving good hugs, making delicious brownies, or telling great bedtime stories but his response was, "You know where to stand." It's actually become a family heirloom story which I repeated at his Bar Mitzvah because although he had been talking about the basketball game, I felt it could also be seen as a metaphor for life because in addition to having compassion and sensitivity for others as well as a good sense of humor, I feel we should always have strong values and know where to stand.

Throughout the often difficult balancing act of combining my multiple roles as mother, wife, physician, and "zoo keeper", I realized very early on that to cope with life's challenges it was important to not only stand firm by one's values but to also know how to laugh and be able to find the humor in situations. It's of course also helpful to always try being able to look on the bright side and fortunately that will usually turn out to be more than just the one lamp in the room.

About the Author

Margie Bessin Peppercorn, M.D. was born and raised in Manhattan and attended Fieldston High School. She graduated Radcliffe College in 1966 and received her M.D. from Harvard Medical School in 1970.

She trained in pediatrics at the Children's Hospital National Medical Center in Washington D.C. and at the Boston City Hospital in Boston, Massachusetts before joining a pediatric group practice in Sudbury Massachusetts where she worked for over 35 years while raising her family and caring for a menagerie of livestock.

She's currently retired but still living in Sudbury with her husband and now just one rabbit.

Made in United States
North Haven, CT
31 December 2022